# The Happy Passion

## A Personal View of Jacob Bronowski

Anthony James

**SOCIETAS**
essays in political
& cultural criticism

**imprint-academic.com**

Published in the UK by Societas
Imprint Academic, PO Box 200, Exeter EX5 5YX, UK

Published in the USA by Societas
Imprint Academic, Philosophy Documentation Center
PO Box 7147, Charlottesville, VA 22906-7147, USA

ISBN 9781845400 2204

A CIP catalogue record for this book is available from the
British Library and US Library of Congress

# Contents

*\* I have scrupulously avoided footnotes in this book because I believe that most non-specialist readers (and, secretly, many specialist readers also) find them rather irritating. However, at the end of the book the reader will find a useful list of books and articles referred to in the text, set down in the order in which I refer to them. A.J.*

For my wife and daughters and

to the memory of my mother.

*Science is a very human form of knowledge. We are always at the brink of the known, we always feel forward for what is to be hoped. Every judgement in science stands on the edge of error, and is personal. Science is a tribute to what we can know although we are fallible*

—Jacob Bronowski

Chapter One

# *Introduction*

*Bronowski's Footprints*

---

If it is possible to say that the underlying pessimism and disillusionment of the last seventy years, particularly the disillusionment with science, originated in a certain place, rather as we say that a certain dance originated in Charleston, then that place might well be Auschwitz. The very name, like that of Hiroshima, and perhaps in recent years the numbers 9/11, is used as a shorthand term to express certain attitudes such as hopelessness and helplessness. The events that these names and numbers represent are also used to justify political actions that are frequently dishonest and political beliefs that are frequently trivial and superficial. The simple truth that these events had causes that can be understood by the use of science and common sense is not nearly so often stated. The pessimism and the disillusionment are still with us today, as I write, and they were certainly with us eleven years ago in 1997 when I visited Auschwitz.

It was a brilliantly sunny day in early July, and we were travelling in a minibus from Krakow to Auschwitz through rich, rolling countryside full of the heavy greens of summer that can give you the oppressive sense of ploughing through an immense salad. Polish villages came and went, and the minibus radio babbled unconcernedly while the driver adjusted his sunglasses and concentrated on the road. There were six passengers in the minibus, four of them German—a couple in their twenties and a couple in their fifties. I dozed at odd moments, with images from the film *Schindler's List* coming back to me. No film can prepare you for Auschwitz, not even the terse and dignified documentary shown before you enter the camp itself, which was watched in shocked or respectful silence by the audience that filled the theatre. The camp appears rather suddenly in the village of Oswiecim and visitors alight in the car park, from which the main gate (not the point of entry for most of those who came to the camp as prisoners) can be seen some distance away. Above the gate is the inscription, mocking and cruel, *ARBEIT MACHT FREI* — Work Makes Free. The funeral march from Beethoven's *Eroica* symphony was played over the film shown to visitors, perhaps as a conscious attempt to show that despite Auschwitz, human civilisation, and Germany as part of that civilisation, goes on.

There were piles, rank upon rank, of empty canisters that had contained Cyclon B crystals that produced the gas for the gas chambers, still bearing the manufacturer's name, Degesch — a firm that made almost 300,000 marks in profits from the sale of the gas between 1941 and 1944. Prisoners came straight off the trains and were subjected to selection for immediate extermination or for work and later death by execution, beating, starvation or illness. Some prisoners died in the gas chambers after later selections. Jews from southern Europe were often told that they would be allowed to begin a new life as farm workers when they were rounded up. To prevent mass panic the SS told people that they would be allowed a shower and must undress, and after this, about two thousand people would be herded into a room of two hundred and ten square metres and the gas would be pumped in. It took about fifteen to twenty minutes to die, after which the gold in the teeth, rings, earrings, and even the hair would be removed from the bodies. The corpses were then burnt in incinerators on the ground floor. At the selections some of the prisoners knew or guessed their fate and there occurred scenes of such anguish and despair that even the SS men had to be given extra rations of vodka in order to continue with their duties. Mothers trying to protect young children were particularly troublesome.

We went into the block that houses the exhibition on the sufferings of Hungarian prisoners, and suddenly the lights failed and we were left to edge our way out in nearly complete darkness. Nothing that could happen in the camp today, perhaps, could have prepared the mind so well for the rest of what we saw. There was a bank of human hair behind a huge glass wall, not a pile or a heap, but a bank, sloping and stretching up and back, thick with dust. If every member of the audience in a large, packed concert hall suddenly had his or her hair shorn off, it would leave something like the amount of hair at which we now stood looking. Here and there, fair hair stood out, including a yellow plait as thick as my wrist. Some nameless yellow-haired girl, such as the poet Yeats might have celebrated, had died crushed together with two thousand others in a chamber two hundred and ten metres square. The efficiency of Heinrich Himmler's planning permeated everything done at Auschwitz. There was a similarly vast array of shoes, boots and sandals, and of cups, tureens and mugs, and of crutches taken from the disabled, artificial limbs, braces taken off children's legs and spectacles. All were to be recycled – the hair was used as fibre in making cloth for instance – in order to provide products for Hitler's Reich. In one block were some of the photographs of the children taken by the SS for the camp records, faces twisted with fear, fresh tears glistening on their cheeks. In a glass case was preserved a little woollen cardigan large enough for a child of three, and in another was a doll with part of its face shattered and the fragments placed carefully beside it. I went down the stairs and outside, unable to stop myself from crying openly and not even trying. A young woman in jeans sat on the steps to this block, trying to collect herself, glancing as numbly at my weeping as she looked at everything else. And yes, it is true, the birds do not sing inside the camp.

I went over to the perimeter fence upon which some of the prisoners killed themselves by throwing themselves on the electrified wire. Although no longer electrified, the wire is still there, as is the barbed wire.

'You have come to a concentration camp, from which the only way to escape is through the crematorium chimney.' Thus, the prisoners who were not immediately selected for the gas chambers on arrival would be informed by the camp supervisor. Large numbers died from hard labour, often performed at a run without respite, and they were subjected to constant casual beatings from the SS and the common criminals who were their assistants. Survivors who have artistic abilities have provided a series of pictures of the daily lives of the prisoners, from reveille through the bowl of soup in the morning to the bowl of soup in the evening, from morning roll call to evening roll call, and above all at work. The overfed common criminals, laughing, leering, swung their sticks and clubs and wounded and maimed emaciated prisoners or beat them to death on the spot. This was not always the case however, because some Germans, convicted as common criminals and given power over ordinary prisoners, behaved with decency and humanity.

The entire camp population was gathered each morning in the assembly square, and morning roll call would often be prolonged for hours, particularly in cold weather. The collective gallows stands here, upon which prisoners who tried to escape or who were accused of some other violation of camp discipline were hanged in the presence of the rest. And in Block 10 the SS Dr C. Clauberg carried out sterilisation experiments on Jewish women and Dr Joseph Mengele experimented on twins and handicapped people. Block 11 is the 'Death Block', and in its courtyard, enclosed by two blocks, is the Wall of Death against which the SS shot thousands of prisoners. The windows of the blocks on either side have wooden blinds and the courtyard is lined with stakes on which prisoners were hung by their arms bent behind their backs. I walked slowly to the wall, in front of which flowers had been placed, and I had intended to touch it, but finally I did not. It seemed too much of an intrusion—a piece of arrogance or impudence. The wall itself did not bring home to me the horror of the murders carried out here, but Block 11 did. When you enter, the room in which the Gestapo Police Court from Katowice convened is on your left, and it is bare and featureless, with a long table at which these men, with their methodical deliberations and documents, sat and pronounced sentence on the prisoners in the rooms on either side of the corridor. In the room on the right the SS officer on duty would await the sentences in readiness to carry them out. Before they were shot, the condemned were made to undress in the two washrooms (male and female) that open onto the courtyard and the Wall of Death. I imagined the waiting, the dread, the terror and the hope of the ordinary human consciousness that cannot believe that it is going to die. Then the call would come, the order, as harsh as it is bored and unconcerned, and then the washroom, the fumbling with the filthy rags that the prisoners wore, and the open door looking onto the courtyard and that wall, and then the final naked steps to the wall. Further down the corridor is the portable gallows, small enough to be loaded onto the back of a small truck, and the whipping stool on which prisoners were flogged, officially twenty-five strokes, usually many more, made of ancient, dark wood, worn smooth.

It slowly became clear to me, as it must to any visitor to Auschwitz, that this camp and all the other similar camps in Nazi Germany were not only factories of death, but also factories of deliberate torment, humiliation and degradation. Millions of ordinary people, Jews, Gypsies, Russians, Czechs, Yugoslavs, French, Austrians, Germans, passed through these camps and were murdered and tormented. And this process was not carried out by a handful of secretive sadists and psychopaths, but by hundreds of thousands of state servants, employees and administrators. The scale of this event and the shadow it has cast on the human consciousness and on humanity's confidence in itself becomes apparent when we reflect on this terrible fact. The cruelty is preserved in intimate detail in the first Auschwitz camp, but in many ways Auschwitz II at Birkenau, about three kilometres away, is even more terrifying, displaying the sheer vast scale of organised murder. The trains loaded with victims rolled right into this factory of death, the site of which stretches into the distance, and today some of the barracks with their floors of compressed earth are still standing. Prisoners would lie six or eight to each tiered level in these monotonous, nameless barracks, containing about a hundred thousand people in August 1944, suffering from lack of water, foul sanitary conditions and an infestation of rats.

The ashes of millions of people were flushed into the pond at Auschwitz, but on that sunny day, as I stood at its edge, brightly coloured insects and tiny frogs skimmed the thick green surface of the water and wild flowers grew nearby. Almost exactly twenty-four years earlier I had sat in front of our television set and watched Dr Jacob Bronowski stand — he declared — as a scientist, a human being, a survivor and a witness at the edge of this pond. Many members of his family had died at Auschwitz. He reminded us that it is said that science will turn people into numbers and told his audience passionately that this is 'false, tragically false', and that it was here in this camp that people were turned into numbers and murdered not by gas ultimately, but by the arrogance, the dogma and the ignorance that unleashed the gas, and by the murderers' own belief that they possessed absolute knowledge, although they had never — unlike scientists — tested their notions against objective reality. During that extraordinary monologue, filmed in one take and not scripted, Bronowski also reminded us that science is a very human form of knowledge in which every judgement stands on the edge of error and is personal. Quoting the words of Oliver Cromwell — 'I beseech you, in the bowels of Christ, think it possible you may be mistaken' — he reached into the water of the pond, telling us that we must close the distance between the push-button order and the human act, and ending with the words: 'We have to touch people.' I deliberately repeated that act of homage in 1997, reaching down and putting my hand in the water of the pond, knowing that the horror I had seen here would never leave me, but also realising that Bronowski's active defiance of failings such as despair, loss of nerve, fashionable pessimism and irresponsibility had made a permanent and indelible impression on me as I had watched it at the age of sixteen.

I had come to Poland in the summer of 1997 for private reasons that were painful and distressing. A relationship that I had believed would last a lifetime had broken up in bitterness and acrimony, and I did not know where my eight year-old daughter was or when, if ever, I would see her again. Four years later, in 2001, my daughter and I had left that anguished and difficult time far behind us, and we were at Thingvellir in Iceland, where the ancient Icelandic parliament began to meet in 930 AD. The vastness and beauty of the Icelandic landscape is difficult to convey — the plain framed by volcanic mountains, the huge lake besides which there is some forest, together with the green but tree-less expanses that remind you that Iceland lies just below the Arctic circle and in the very furthest north within it, and the incredibly sharp and jagged walls and cliff tops of the Almannagja gorge, into which at one point there is the inex-orable, downward-crashing, white water of Oxarafoss Falls. The walls of the gorge form a natural amphitheatre, and there, the Althing, the whole Norse community assem-bled as a parliament, met each year to make laws and settle disputes in a setting more impressive than that used by any democratic assembly in history — a hall that was not built by human beings but by geology. Bronowski had ended programme eleven of his television series *The Ascent of Man* at Auschwitz with the moving and dignified appeal that I have described above. He began programme thirteen, the final episode of the series, at Thingvellir in Iceland with a celebration of democracy and justice, and I could not help reflecting that from a personal standpoint my visit to Auschwitz had coincided with one of the worst times in my own life, just as my visit to Thingvellir coincided with one of the happiest. Also, I felt that another place in the world that would live in my memory for the rest of my life had — so to speak — Bronowski's footprints upon it. I had seen Thingvellir on our television screen at sixteen, just as I had seen Auschwitz.

Bronowski pointed out as he stood at Thingvellir that the existence of the Icelandic parliament before the coming of Christianity, 'at a time when China was a great empire, and Europe was the spoil of princelings and robber barons', is a remarkable beginning to democracy. He then made the startling statement that justice is part of the biological equipment of human beings because of a biological feature that is unique to human beings (species-specific) – the fact that while other animals are either social or solitary, we aspire to be both in one, a social solitary. Justice is the tight-rope that we walk between our desire to fulfil our wishes and our acknowledgement of our social responsibility: so Bronowski told us with a characteristic flourish of clarity and elegance. If he had lived longer and if his series of 'tele-vision essays' had been made later, he might have added the insights provided by Richard Leakey and Roger Lewin in their book *Origins Reconsidered* (1992) in which they refer to extensive research on primates. Human beings at an early stage of evolution, like the primates we can observe today, lived in extended social groups in which individuals com-peted for sexual favours, a greater share of the food supply, prestige and status. The ability to foresee what your com-petitor will do next greatly increases success in this elabo-rate social chess game, and to predict well you need to imagine what he/she is feeling as if you were feeling it yourself, so that this is the biological basis and the begin-ning of compassion and sympathy, of 'feeling with', and thus also the basis of morality generally.

Bronowski's *The Ascent of Man* is arguably the greatest achievement in documentary television in the history of that medium, and it was first screened in the 1970s. The social upheavals and transformations of the previous decade, the sixties, still permeated everything, and the smell of the sixties was still in the air: unprecedented pros-perity and sexual freedom in the West, a new independence for the young and an antagonism between the generations, anti-war protests, LSD, a new kind of popular music, flower power, hippies, the increasing assertion of equality and freedom on the part of women and oppressed racial groups, and above them all the incredible spectacle of human beings on the Moon and the looming terror of nuclear war — something for which to blame scientists and something for which to praise them. Everyone tends to overrate the significance of his or her own era, and perhaps I am overestimating the extraordinary quality of the 1970s because I grew to adulthood in that decade. However, in the 1970s a civil war broke out on the streets of Northern Ireland, defined by the British government as part of the United Kingdom, and the United States suffered the first defeat in war in its history at the hands of Vietnam. In 1972 a great American actress, Jane Fonda, flew to Vietnam to talk with and mix with the soldiers and leaders of a country at war with her own, and in 1974 a Russian writer, Solzhenitsyn, defied the Soviet government and was deported to the West because his books terrified the Soviet leaders and his fame prevented them from imprisoning or killing him. In the same year, 1974, the American President Richard Nixon resigned to avoid impeachment and an Afro-American boxer, Muhammad Ali, by then a symbol and a legend, regained the heavyweight championship of the world in, of all places, the African state of Zaire. In April 1970 the spacecraft carrying three American astronauts to the Moon sustained severe damage and the crew were brought home in an episode of almost unbelievable courage and ingenuity, and in June 1976 an automated spacecraft landed on the surface of Mars and sent back high resolution images, detailed colour photographs from the surface of another planet. In 1970 an Australian academic and Shakespearean scholar called Germaine Greer published a book titled *The Female Eunuch* and became in the eyes of the media and the public — if not always in the eyes of other feminists — a charismatic, sexy and popular icon of feminism, and in 1979 a right-wing Conservative, Margaret Thatcher, became the first woman Prime Minister of Britain and proceeded to dismantle the society that had existed in Britain since 1945. It was a decade of confusing, conflicting and competing voices, but in *The Ascent of Man*, first screened in 1973, and in the last radio broadcasts that were heard in 1975, after his death,

Bronowski's voice spoke out clearly and became one of the
defining influences of that decade.

Firstly, Bronowski was sure that human history *is an
ascent*, although there was nothing facile or sentimental in
his conviction, as I think the views he expressed at the pond
in Auschwitz quoted above clearly demonstrate. In his own
eyes he had lived through the two worst disasters of the
twentieth century—the rise of Hitler and the use of the
atomic bomb against Japan. He consistently and passionately defended the integrity and value of science, and he
rightly insisted that scientific knowledge could only be pursued—science could only be 'done'—by an act of the imagination, and he saw the scientific imagination and the artistic
imagination as complementary, flowing together to form
the supreme achievement of the human species. He was
scornful of the silly and falsely profound inferences drawn
from certain kinds of research—although not of the
research itself—the kind of inferences that are still popular
today, and he was well aware that biology has been invoked
at least since the nineteenth century to justify predatory
wars and callous economics. Although he would be saddened to find that those justifications are still being used
today, thirty-four years after his death, he would hardly be
surprised. He constantly reminded us that our unique qualities as human beings are far more interesting and significant than the qualities we share with rats and pigeons,
indeed there must be something unique about us, 'because
otherwise, evidently, the ducks would be lecturing about
Konrad Lorenz, and the rats would be writing papers about
B.F. Skinner.' The faintly Eastern European wit and
humour, always thoroughly intellectual, were ever present!
Bronowski was a fierce opponent of the perpetuation of the
'two cultures' of literature and science as mutually incomprehensible and opposed, although he admitted that scientists were partly to blame for creating this atmosphere. He
wrote superb literary criticism and he wrote poetry, elabo-
rating a philosophy that identified two kinds of knowledge,
insisting that the knowledge brought to us by literature is as
valid and important as the knowledge brought to us by sci-

ence, repeating in the Foreword to the book of *The Ascent of Man* that his ambition in that work had been the same as in all his other books: 'to create a philosophy for the twentieth century which shall be all of one piece.' He was a short, stocky, robust man, full of jokes and charm, with a kindly face and round spectacles and a high forehead, striding across the television screen in the early 1970s (by then he had already been a radio and television personality for more than two decades) radiating optimism and a sense of the excitement and adventure of being human and able to think.

Many of us are influenced by a variety of famous people and cultural figures when we are young, and then our perceptions of these figures change, rather as our feelings about a parent, a wife, a husband or a lover change. At first there is a fair amount of idealisation and idolisation, but later there follows a wary acknowledgement of the faults of the individual who has made such an impact upon us, although a certain respect and admiration may remain. For myself, I retain a limited and qualified respect for Churchill and for Lenin, for Solzhenitsyn and for the great anarchist Emma Goldman, but if I had to name those individuals who have excited my imagination and for whom my admiration is largely undiminished because their influence on the world has been almost entirely positive and benign, I would certainly include Dr Jacob Bronowski. (It would be a very personal, subjective and eclectic list, but for the record I would also include the Russian poet Anna Akhmatova and the former President of the Republic of Ireland Mary Robinson, but perhaps no others.)

This short book has been written in the year that marks the hundredth anniversary of Bronowski's birth, and is an expanded version of my article *ENDURING OPTIMISM: An Appreciation of Jacob Bronowski*. It is not an assessment of his work as a scientist or a full-scale biography, neither of which I am competent to produce, but it does attempt to give an account of Bronowski as a philosopher and of Bronowski as a historian of science and culture generally. However, this account of him cannot begin to compete, in

breadth and excitement and sheer readability, with
Bronowski's own books (he was always readable and accessible and he meant to be, writing to be understood, which is
not a universal quality among philosophers), but nevertheless, this little book may give a summary and an overview of
his best books and his best ideas and it is aimed at the
non-specialist and the interested general reader. I continue
to believe — perhaps on insufficient grounds — that books
and ideas can help the world. Bronowski himself certainly
believed this and he also believed in 'the democracy of the
intellect', not as an academic nicety, but as a condition for
the survival of society and civilisation. Democracy, of
course, means the right to choose, to listen or to ignore, to
decide what is relevant, and therefore, we can only blame
ourselves if we ignore individuals like Bronowski and the
message they bring.

Chapter Two

# Full Heart and Full Mind

*The Life*

A full-scale biography of Jacob Bronowski may soon be written, or perhaps is already being written, and the varied life of such a fascinating man, bound up as it was with some of the crucial events of the last hundred years and of all human history, would make the best sort of material for the biographer's art and would teach us a good deal about our own culture. However, as I have previously stated, this book is a personal view of Bronowski as a philosopher. Nevertheless, I do wish to give the main outlines of his life because we cannot appreciate his thinking properly without such an impression, and above all, I want to place him in the context of the times he lived through and of cultural history generally. This chapter draws upon the information about Bronowski's life published since his death, and occasionally quotes from those who knew him, as well as using the autobiographical passages in his own books and broadcasts — really quite numerous for a scientist and a philosopher — to fill out the picture.

Jacob Bronowski was born in Lodz in Poland on January 18 1908, the son of Abram Bronowski and Celia Flatto. His father owned a haberdashery firm that traded with London, and he seems to have been an intelligent, though not well-educated man, but — as Jacob later described him —

he was learned in the Old Testament and its commentaries, he tried to keep up with the news, but if he had been asked to give an outline of what he knew in science, it would have been rather muddled.

He also recalls (coming up with both these reminiscences in the last radio broadcasts, interviews with George Steedman, *Journey Round a Twentieth Century Skull*) that by the time he was a few years old the word 'relativity' was on everybody's tongue as a consequence of Einstein's early work. The influence of that work spread into every area of knowledge, creating the awareness that social relations, relations between men and women, religions, the place of human beings in nature are all relative, and it was a particularly twentieth-century idea, destroying the old fixed absolutes. Bronowski spent much of his life expounding the implications of that idea, and it is, of course, a concept that is as central as ever in the twenty-first century, although it is sometimes lazily vulgarised in order to justify avoiding choice and responsibility, or sometimes simply ignored.

Bronowski's family emigrated from Poland to Germany when Russia brought that part of Poland under full military occupation during the First World War, and although Poland had been partitioned between Russia, Austria and Prussia (transformed into a united Germany in 1871) and had ceased to exist as an independent state since the eighteenth century, most Poles saw the rule of Tsarist Russia as the worst of alternatives. The fact that the Bronowski family preferred to live in Imperial Germany in wartime may reflect the fear held by Eastern Europeans — especially Eastern European Jews — at the prospect of Tsarist rule, especially full military occupation. Fear of the destruction that would follow from closeness to full-scale military operations was doubtless also a factor, and the family were to remain in Germany through the war. After its defeat in 1918, a large degree of chaos, unrest and social upheaval spread across Germany, and this was perhaps the cause of a second move by the family in 1920, this time to London. In *The Common Sense of Science* Bronowski describes landing in England as a boy of twelve, able to speak only two words of

English, badly pronounced, that he had learned on the channel boat, and later being unable to read English easily for another two or three years. He adds that he read 'greedily, with excitement, with affection, with a perpetual sense of discovering a new and, I slowly realized, a great literature.' Interestingly, he recalls that the two writers in whom he was able to discern literary style were Macaulay and Joseph Conrad. Bronowski's great handicap as a boy was that he knew no English history, and therefore he could not put the great mass of books and writers to which his relentless reading led him into any kind of order or context. He seems never to have forgotten this early disadvantage, and by an intuitive leap he has identified it as the chief difficulty experienced by the ordinary person in trying to acquire an understanding of science — scientific discoveries need a context, we need to know *why* they were important enough to change the world in our own time and in previous historical periods. The intention behind most of Bronowski's work was to provide that context.

In his superb book on Nietzsche, J.P. Stern begins with a consideration of 'Nietzsche in Company', comparing and contrasting the influence of Nietzsche with that of Karl Marx and Sigmund Freud, the other two thinkers who have shaped the modern outlook. Perhaps I can pause at this point and try to emulate J. P. Stern's example by considering 'Bronowski in Company', although from a narrower perspective. There are two other supremely gifted writers who came from Eastern and Central Europe to Britain in the space of less than forty years, the novelist Joseph Conrad and the historian Eric Hobsbawm, and like Bronowski they wrote in English. Conrad was the son of a Polish nobleman who was exiled to Siberia by the Russians for his nationalist activities, and he settled in Britain a quarter of a century before Bronowski's arrival, leaving a career as a captain in the British Merchant Service to become one of the greatest novelists in English literature and world literature. Conrad, like Bronowski, enthusiastically embraced the tolerant atmosphere of Britain, but unlike Bronowski, he remained a profoundly pessimistic and conservative writer (perhaps nihilistic would ultimately be a better description), and more important than these contrasts, he began to reflect that shift in outlook and consciousness in the new twentieth century — that 'relativity' that was on everybody's tongue when Bronowski was only a few years old — except that his novels started to reflect this before Einstein had been heard of, in fact almost before any other writer. There is no absolute 'truth' in Conrad's novels, as there was in earlier fiction, but instead there are the overlapping perspectives of a number of characters, varying according to their viewpoint, and each of them contributing something. Eric Hobsbawm was born to an Austrian mother and a father who was a London Jewish cabinet-maker, a British subject, in 1917, after the couple had been given special permission as subjects of countries at war (Britain and Austria) to marry in Zurich. He first visited Britain in 1929 (at the same age as Bronowski when he arrived in London), moving to Britain permanently in 1933, a few months after Hitler came to power, but arriving as a British subject, just as he had lived as one in Berlin in the last days before Hitler's rule. Hobsbawm was a Marxist from his early youth, and as such he was somewhat less enthusiastic about British culture than Conrad and Bronowski, and he was also a member of the Communist Party for decades. He never allowed his membership to compromise the integrity of his great historical works, or to prevent him from publicly protesting against outrages such as the Soviet invasion of Hungary in 1956. All three of these writers, in their very different ways, pursued within the atmosphere of British culture, with its regard for law and freedom of expression, a very Central European and un-English seriousness on a massive scale, a preoccupation with ideas and with an encompassing philosophy for the modern world. It should be added that Hobsbawm attended Cambridge a few years after Bronowski. The three writers also had a very *democratic* faith in ideas and in telling the truth (artistic truth only for the pessimistic Conrad) that was peculiarly Central European in its flavour, however favourable Britain was for its growth, and we should remember that Britain remained a haven for politically oppressed exiles, Karl Marx included, until just after the Second World War.

Bronowski gained admission to the Central Foundation Boys' School in London despite his difficulties, developing an equal interest in both science and literature, and winning a mathematics scholarship to Jesus College, Cambridge. He was a Wrangler (First Class) in Part I of the mathematical tripos in 1928 and Senior Wrangler (ranked top of the list of First Class students) in Part II of the mathematical tripos in 1930. Also at Cambridge, he edited a literary magazine called *Experiment* — a title that bridges the literary and the scientific in a fashion typical of him — together with William Empson, another mathematician later famous as a literary critic, and Humphrey Jennings, a film-maker. He later recalled the exhilaration of intellectual life in Cambridge in those years and the developments in quantum physics, splitting the atom and the discovery of the neutron, combined with innovation in literature and painting and the new maturity and confidence in film and radio productions. In his last broadcasts *Journey Round a Twentieth Century Skull*, Bronowski gives two anecdotes that convey the flavour of his time in Cambridge in the early 1930s. In the first he recalls a party he attended at which the name John Cockcroft was mentioned, followed by someone else asking what was so special about Cockcroft. The answer was that Cockcroft had split the atom and was exultantly going around and slapping everybody on the shoulders and declaring that it had been done with an old tobacco tin and some neutrons — 'and the Americans have been spending millions.' In the second recollection Bronowski describes Albert Einstein receiving an honorary degree at Cambridge, flanked on one side by the poet W.B. Yeats, 'a noble-looking man' and on the other by Gowland Hopkins, the founder of modern biochemistry. 'That conjunction of the arts and the sciences was the most natural thing in the world.'

After the award of his first degree, Bronowski carried out research into problems of geometry, receiving his doctorate in 1935 for work on algebraic geometry. This was an extraordinary achievement, by anyone's standards, for a young man who had stepped ashore in England at the age of twelve unable to speak English, and it may remind us of the award of the Nobel Prize for Literature to the French novelist Albert Camus, the son of an itinerant farm labourer who died when Camus was an infant, and of an illiterate charwoman. Bronowski was not, however, at all modest about his achievements, and he radiated supreme self-confidence, and yet it is fair to ask *why should* this decent, kindly and democratic man, who advocated the democracy of the intellect and gave most of his life to educating the public, have affected modesty and reticence about his own abilities? Would such a pose have made him a better person, scientist or philosopher? In 1932 he embarked on an adventure in which he would have found modesty of little use to him, and through this episode there emerges a picture of Bronowski that is considerably different from the one that most of us are used to, although it helps us to understand the constant presence of wit and fun in the work of his later life. His interest in poetry was intense enough for him to accept an invitation from the poet Laura Riding to visit her in her home in Deya, Mallorca. Bronowski was wary of being alone with Riding and so begged his companion Eirlys Roberts, a Classics student at Cambridge, 'a thin, quiet, good-looking girl', to accompany him. The painful and funny times that followed are vividly conveyed in two biographies of the poet Robert Graves (who was living in Deya with Laura Riding at this time), *Robert Graves: His Life and Work* by Martin Seymour-Smith (1982, revised 1995) and *Robert Graves: Life on the Edge* by Miranda Seymour (1995), both of which I have drawn upon. I have also used *Robert Graves: The Years with Laura 1926–40* by Richard Perceval Graves (1990). The biographies largely agree on the incidents in which Bronowski was involved.

Laura Riding, an American poet, was born in 1901, and Robert Graves, an English poet, in 1895. She was a poet of genius, possessing a unique style, and was also obsessed with truth and by doubts about whether poetry (including her own) was of any use in getting at the truth about human existence, doubts that were to lead her to abandon poetry altogether as she grew older. Clearly, a writer such as Riding must start with formidable intelligence and integrity, yet it seems that Riding was often tyrannous, cruel, intolerant of any opinions other than her own and suspicious to the point of paranoia. Riding met Graves in 1926, and they later lived in Deya, Mallorca until 1936, so that their departure preceded the disintegration of their relationship in 1940. Robert Graves was also a poet of immense gifts, with a dedication to poetry and a sense of reverence at its special quality that perhaps no other poet writing in English in the last hundred and fifty years has possessed. He was also tormented throughout his life by his terrible experiences as a frontline soldier in the First World War and by his deeply unhappy childhood. Graves seems to have been extremely submissive to Riding during their Mallorca years, but they both—though perhaps less obviously Graves during that period—wanted acolytes, courtiers, or at best secretaries. There have been bitter quarrels between supporters, literary scholars and journalists over the reputations and the characters of Riding and Graves in recent years. This bare statement of the facts gives some idea of the environment that the young Jacob was about to enter.

Bronowski and Eirlys Roberts visited Deya in the summer of 1932, staying for several weeks. Graves described Bronowski as 'a young Polish Jew who is really a geometrician at Cambridge and has a very good mind.' Yet behind the apparent compliment there seems to have lurked the intention to demean Bronowski, since—according to one of the sources used by Richard Perceval Graves—Bronowski was hardly just a geometrician, and his stature as an all-round mathematician was indisputable, as Graves probably knew very well. If it was the intention of Graves to demean Bronowski, then there was reason for it. Even Laura Riding, who had invited him, was less than pleased by his air of intellectual superiority, and Bronowski succeeded in making Robert Graves extremely uneasy by his self-confidence in general and particularly by his challenge to Graves to compete with him at writing ballads or nursery rhymes. Clearly, the celebrated poet aged thirty-seven with so many upper class connections was upset by the 'geometrician' aged twenty-four, and understandably Graves liked Eirlys much more, although he ignored the single factual error she pointed out in his novel about ancient Rome. Eirlys seems to have been more perceptive than Bronowski in noticing how detached Graves was and how his mind was always on his work, whatever task he was performing, and she was later able to foresee that he would survive his destructive relationship with Laura Riding by retreating into his inner world. Despite these tensions, Jacob and Eirlys seemed to enjoy their visit enough to promise to return after leaving Cambridge the following summer. Riding wrote to Bronowski quite often in the following months, about her writing, her plans and projects, and about her health, which, in common with many poets, she complained was bad.

Bronowski returned to Deya in autumn 1933 with Eirlys, setting to work with Laura Riding on a journal called *The Critical Vulgate* — a journal that would pronounce on values and truth, giving expression to preoccupations that were typical of Riding. All seems to have gone well at first, and the celebrations at New Year were uproarious, with Bronowski singing a jolly, rousing Russian song that was appreciated by the others, although none of them could understand the words. Bronowski's performance was only outshone by that of another friend of Riding and Graves, Mary Ellidge, who at the party given for the birthday of Graves in July 1934, stripped down to her green silk camiknickers and sitting astride a chair in a provocative way, sang a Marlene Dietrich song. By the September of that year, *I, Claudius*, the novel Graves had written about ancient Rome, had achieved very large sales and received ecstatic reviews, and Graves seems to have dutifully and generously used his financial success to support Riding and her career. Riding, however, was not appreciative, and instead was outright jealous. These feelings may have contributed to her final break with Bronowski in that September, taking the form of a monumental row in which she told him that he was a bad character and he replied that she 'was no lily-white angel' (apparently this remark became legend-ary). The underlying reason for the quarrel was that Bronowski wanted equality in his collaboration with Rid-ing and was sick of her telling him what to do, as well as resenting her badly informed pronouncements on science and her attempts to edit his own poems — all of which he pointed out to her forcefully. Bronowski and Eirlys were on their way back to England within hours of the quarrel, leav-ing Riding behind with Graves, who loathed Bronowski enough to write a satirical poem about him called 'Jacob's Ladder', although he had been unwilling to declare his dis-like to Jacob's face as long as the 'geometrician' remained in favour with Riding. There is one further reference to Bronowski in the biography of Graves by Martin Seymour-Smith regarding the indignation of Graves over the Suez invasion by Britain in 1956, when the poet found himself contradicted by a friend of his called James Reeves. Seymour-Smith states that it was Bronowski who had influ-enced Reeves in his pro-government opinions. In a letter? In a conversation? Such views seem unlikely ones for Bronowski to hold, given his known convictions about war, politics and race. However, Seymour-Smith does not give any source or date for Bronowski's 'influence' on Reeves, which seems to me to be a lapse that falls below the usual high standard and integrity of his work. Of the three books I have drawn upon in describing the Riding-Bronowski asso-ciation, the one by Richard Perceval Graves is the most sym-pathetic to Bronowski. The strange adventure in Deya, Mallorca was now decidedly over, and it may have strengthened both the balance between poetic knowledge and scientific knowledge that Bronowski looked for throughout his life and also his dislike of elitism and 'the aristocracy of the intellect' as he was later to call it.

Bronowski recalled late in his life how as a teenager he had walked on Saturday afternoons from London's East End to the British Museum, in order to look at a single statue brought there from Easter Island, and that he had grown up indifferent to the division between literature and sci-ence — 'the two languages for experience that I learned together.' Clearly, in Deya with Riding and Graves, poetry had been idolised at the expense of science, and finally Bronowski had come to distrust the kind of poetic language that Riding used. It must have seemed to him that it was time to restore the balance, and he accepted an appointment as a lecturer in mathematics at University College, Hull later in 1934, and subsequently was promoted to senior lecturer. In 1933, before his second stay in Deya he had published a solution of the classical functional Waring problem and had also become a British citizen. At that time Hull awarded University of London external degrees. It was here that Bronowski continued his research into geometry, publishing a series of papers *On triple planes* and *The figure of six points in space of four dimensions*, but it was typical of his career that his first published book was *The Poet's Defence* (1939).

Bronowski married Rita Coblentz, a sculptor, in 1941, and his wife later recalled that they were married early on a Monday morning during a daylight air raid on London. The air raid was perhaps ironically significant because the couple were to live in Hull only until the following year, 1942, when they moved to secret locations because of Bronowski's war work, which included pioneering methods of operational research that used mathematics to increase the effectiveness of bombing raids and their economic impact. Ultimately, Bronowski was as involved with *waging war* as any frontline soldier or pilot, and he never seems to have been tempted by the pacifism of some intellectuals of the thirties and forties, perhaps because he never failed to perceive clearly the extent of the evil intrinsic in Nazism, one of 'the two great catastrophes of the twentieth century', as he called it in his last broadcasts – the other being the *use* of the atomic bomb in 1945. He also reminded us, late in his career, how the 'progress in nuclear physics and the march of Hitler went step by step, pace by pace, in a way that we forget now.' Today, it might be added that as late as the beginning of 1943 victory over Hitler was still very, very uncertain, as a number of excellent historians such as Paul Addison and Laurence Rees have reminded us in the last few years. Thus, Bronowski never opposed the *making* of the atomic bomb — scientists during the war were haunted by the possibility that Hitler might acquire one first — but, like his friend Leo Szilard, who worked on the development of this weapon, he opposed its use against the Japanese in 1945, which was not inevitable or necessary.

In *The Ascent of Man* Bronowski gives an account of working with the famous mathematician Johnny von Neumann that gives us something of the flavour of his wartime work. The two scientists were looking at a mathematical problem arising from the photograph of an explosion, and von Neumann told Bronowski that he did not have the right kind of imagination to see the solution. As we have noticed, Bronowski was not a modest man, but he seems to have been capable of considerable patience and humility in the company of those whose knowledge he respected, and — unlike the encounter with Laura Riding — no quarrel with von Neumann ensued. Instead, von Neumann went off to London and Bronowski went to his laboratory at a secret location in the darkened, air-raid-wary English countryside and worked until about midnight, only to find that von Neumann was right. Knowing that his colleague always slept late, Bronowski waited until well after ten in the morning to telephone him and tell him that he was right. Answering the phone in bed, von Neumann said: 'You wake me up early in the morning to tell me that I'm right? Please wait until I'm wrong.'

Bronowski and Rita had four daughters, and it is also in *The Ascent of Man* that he describes tiptoeing to the cradle of his first daughter and reflecting: 'These marvellous fingers, every joint so perfect, down to the finger nails. I could not have designed that detail in a million years.' Less idyllically, though no doubt realistically, Bronowski's daughter Lisa Jardine said in a recent interview that she was lucky she was a girl and would probably have had a nervous breakdown if she had been a boy, 'the gender difference meant that my father never felt threatened by me and I never wanted to be him.' She has, of course, become a distinguished public intellectual in her own right. Bronowski seems to have enjoyed an unusually happy marriage, and two friends, Eric and Freda Roll, recalled after his death that he would send a card each Christmas to those he cared about bearing a new poem by him and a drawing by his wife.

In 1945 Bronowski went to Japan as Scientific Deputy to the British Chiefs of Staff Mission to study the effects of the atomic bomb, an experience he describes in some detail at the beginning of his book *Science and Human Values* (1956). Landing on an airstrip in the south of Japan on a fine day in November 1945, Bronowski was taken by jeep through the mountains and pine forests to a ship anchored in Nagasaki Harbour. He tells us that he knew nothing of the country or the distance involved as dusk fell on the evening of that day, only realising that he had reached Nagasaki when he heard the ship's loudspeakers playing dance music.

> I had blundered into this desolate landscape [...] the warm night and the meaningless shapes [...] the skeletons of the Mitsubishi factory buildings pushed backwards and side-ways as if by a giant hand [...] a concrete power house with its roof punched in [...] cockeyed telegraph posts and loops of wire in a waste of ashes.

Nagasaki had, ironically, been the home of the largest Christian community in Japan, and in it forty thousand people died in a flash lasting a few seconds. Bronowski states that the idea for his book came to him at the moment of his arrival in the city, which had been an industrial slum before the atomic bomb was dropped and was an 'ashy desolation' when he set foot in it; and he uses the title of the dance song that was played on the ship's loudspeakers to conclude superbly the first section of the book: 'civilization asks of both ruins, *Is You Is Or Is You Ain't Ma Baby?*'.

Bronowski wrote his famous scientific report *The Effects of the Atomic Bombs at Hiroshima and Nagasaki* after his return from Japan—the definitive British scientific document on the bombings. A second book on poetry, *William Blake, a Man Without a Mask* had been published in 1944, written in the hours when he was not engaged in scientific work for the war effort. The scientific posts he now began to occupy, from the end of the war onwards, multiplied and over-lapped strikingly. Between 1945 and 1950 he was engaged in statistical research for the government, applying mathematical models of analysis and forecasting to industry and the economy, and during these years, in 1947, he also served for a time as head of the Projects Division of UNESCO. In 1950, he was appointed Director of the Coal Research Establishment of the National Coal Board and as Director-General of Process Development for the Board between 1959 and 1963 he carried out research into the making of smokeless fuel, overseeing the development and production of this fuel, known as 'Bronowski's Bricks'. During his years with the Coal Board, in 1953, he was on leave of absence as Carnegie Visiting Professor to the Massachusetts Institute of Technology, where he first presented the chapters of his book *Science and Human Values* as a series of lectures. Bronowski also wrote a radio drama called *The Face of Violence*, awarded the Italia Prize for the best dramatic work broadcast throughout Europe in 1950 and 1951 (later published in 1954), and through the forties, fifties and early sixties he established his reputation as firstly a radio personality and later a television personality, appearing frequently on the famous radio programme *The Brains Trust*. It is not an exaggeration to say that cultural history offers few examples of such a combination in one career of professional science, responsible administrative positions, poetry, philosophy, success in drama, popularity and public esteem. One of the few parallels that springs readily to mind is the German poet Goethe, who described himself as having been born under 'a happy constellation', words that Bronowski was to echo in speaking of himself towards the end of his life, and perhaps only happy individuals are capable of such wide-ranging and relentless activity.

The year 1950 marked a turning point in Bronowski's career more profound than the beginning of his research into smokeless fuel for the Coal Board. In his last broadcasts he recalls being asked to call at the office of the anthropologist Le Gros Clark, which he duly did, sitting there flirting with the anthropologist's secretary. Le Gros Clark asked

Bronowski to come and look at some teeth, although Bronowski 'was having a very good time looking at *her* [the secretary's] teeth'. The teeth were those in the fossilised skull of an *Australopithecus* hominid child found at Taung in Africa, dating from more than two million years ago. Bronowski, a specialist in abstract mathematics about the shapes of objects, was asked to make calculations based on the size of the teeth combined with their shape in order to distinguish them, with certainty, from the teeth of apes. The calculations worked 'pretty well' and he experienced a new excitement about his own knowledge and about the human past and human identity that was to remain with him for the rest of his life, finding himself now

> totally committed to thinking about what makes man what he is: in the scientific work I have done since then, the literature I have written, and in these programmes (*The Ascent of Man*).

Bronowski had already in 1960 become a non-resident fellow at the new Salk Institute for Biological Studies at La Jolla, San Diego, California, running parallel with his presentation of the television series *Insight* for the BBC in the early 1960s, in which he examined scientific and mathematical concepts such as entropy, probability and also the nature of human intelligence. In January 1964, with his commitment as Director-General of Process Development for the Coal Board finally behind him, he became resident at the Salk Institute in La Jolla when he was made Senior Fellow, finally becoming Director of the Council for Biology in Human Affairs at the Institute in 1970. His time at the Salk Institute took him away from television and radio appearances in Britain for a period of about ten years. The BBC nevertheless invited him to present a television series tracing the development of science, and in accepting he quickly widened the concept to become a personal view of human cultural evolution, writing the first outline of *The Ascent of Man* in July 1969, and significantly, at 9.56 pm, Houston time, on the twentieth of that month, Neil Armstrong became the first human being to step onto the 'magnificent desolation' (as his companion Edwin Aldrin called it) of the

Moon's surface. Filming of the thirteen television essays began in July 1971 and the last footage was shot in December 1972, a project demanding 'unflagging intellectual and physical vigour, a total immersion' as Bronowski recalled in his Foreword to the book version. Thus, he returned to British television screens in the summer of 1973, wonderfully fulfilling the ambition he had pursued in his other books, 'to create a philosophy for the twentieth century which shall be all of one piece.' The programmes have been watched by millions of viewers, when they were first screened and since, including myself, aged sixteen in the summer of 1973, awaiting each episode with desperate eagerness. The series won him the Royal Television Society's silver medal for outstanding creative achievement.

Towards the end of the series, in the last essay, Bronowski sounded a more pessimistic word of warning about the 'terrible loss of nerve' he sensed in Western society, a retreat into 'Zen Buddhism, into falsely profound questions about, Are we not really just animals at bottom; into extra-sensory perception and mystery'. If he were alive today, Bronowski might add religious fundamentalism and intolerance, a new and aggressive colonialism, and the confident labelling and demonising of each other on the part of human societies to his list. About two years after Bronowski recorded these words the Russian writer Alexander Solzhenitsyn launched his own series of attacks on Western society, against its godless humanism, complacency and lack of political and military determination in the face of the (alleged) threat of Soviet conquest. Solzhenitsyn's attacks were understandable in terms of his own background and life history but, although they contributed to an unfortunate change of attitude in American ruling circles, they had little relevance to his listeners, whereas Bronowski's warnings seem as relevant as ever.

Tragically, the 'total immersion' in the making of a series that demanded two years of creative effort and visiting more than thirty countries was to take its toll, making Bronowski ill during the production of the series, and causing his health to worsen after its completion. He died of a heart attack on Long Island, New York on August 22 1974, aged sixty-six. It must surely have been a cruel blow for his family and his friends, and even outside that circle, for ordinary members of his audience like myself, the loss was unusually sharp: at the time when he seemed most with us, when his fame and his achievement were at their highest, and his voice more needed than ever, he was suddenly gone. His remains were buried in Highgate Cemetery, London, where stands the tomb of Karl Marx, another who also came to Britain as a foreigner, and spent much of his creative life there, also seeking a philosophy that would be all of one piece.

After completing *The Ascent of Man* Bronowski recorded his last radio broadcasts, *Journey Round a Twentieth Century Skull*, interviews with George Steedman. He also appeared on television with the famous British interviewer Michael Parkinson. In his autobiography Parkinson observes that Bronowski's replies were 'beautifully constructed prose' to which the audience listened 'spellbound'. Engagingly, Parkinson asked Bronowski finally if anyone should listen to anything he said. Bronowski replied that people should listen to him, not because they should necessarily believe him,

> but because you have to be pleased there are people who have lived happy and complete lives, who feel they can speak out of a full heart and a full mind, all in the same frame.

Chapter Three

# Bronowski at Work

*The Philosophy*

I have given the third and longest chapter of this short book a very ordinary and everyday title, and this might have pleased Bronowski. Anyone who has stayed with me as far as this should not be daunted or put off by the need to consider Bronowski as a philosopher. Jacob Bronowski wrote to be understood and wanted his books to reach anyone who possessed a normal curiosity about the world, so any book that summarises his work needs to be equally accessible. In this chapter I shall range over six of his best books as well as his final broadcasts, *Journey Round a Twentieth Century Skull*. I shall concentrate on *The Common Sense of Science* (1951), *Science and Human Values* (1956), *The Identity of Man* (1965), *The Origins of Knowledge and Imagination* (1978, a series of lectures given in 1967 and published posthumously), *The Ascent of Man* (1973) and *The Visionary Eye* (1978, compiled and edited by Piero E. Ariotti and Rita Bronowski). In considering these books I shall make divisions and connections that were not necessarily Bronowski's own, but which seem helpful in summarising his work for readers today, as well as referring to other books and articles of his when this seems appropriate. Inevitably, there will be a certain amount of repetition in this chapter, but hopefully, in repeating key statements and ideas I will also expand on them and give them due emphasis. Bronowski himself showed remarkable consistency in his work from *The Common Sense of Science* in 1951 to his last books, and when he repeated his ideas he also enlarged upon them.

As we have already seen, Bronowski wanted 'to create a philosophy for the twentieth century which shall be all of one piece'. I believe that he succeeded. I believe that he created both a philosophy of science and a scientific philosophy as well as something of even greater value: a philosophy of human identity, of what we *are*, and of what we *do* in the world that makes us unique—that is, exercise imagination to make discoveries and build up knowledge. Our greatest achievement as a species is the construction of art and the construction of science *together*, each complementing the other as the greatest sources of knowledge that we have; although art gives us one kind of knowledge and science gives us another kind, both are of equal value and equal significance. Bronowski never lost sight of this fact and he never tired of communicating it to others in his work. Above I have used the word *construction*—that is, science is something we construct, it is 'no less, and no more, personal than any other form of communicated thought', as Bronowski put it in the first of his books to be considered in this chapter. *Hamlet* and *Middlemarch* and *Ulysses* and *The Golden Notebook* are all stamped indelibly with the style and personality of the individuals who wrote them, and so for that matter are *Das Kapital* and *The Communist Manifesto*. Isaac Newton and Einstein and Stephen Hawking in their work have no less of a *personal style* of their own. Science is not some kind of sharp scalpel that can be used by clever people to simply slice open the surface of the world so that all the inner workings are revealed just as they are, on full view, indisputably and forever. Instead, science is a picture of the world, a model—although it deals in what can be measured, tested, quantified in a way that art does not. Further, just as no work of art, not even *Hamlet* or Beethoven's Ninth Symphony, is perfect, so also no scientific description of the world is ever the last word, the final conclusive account of how nature works, although in the seventeenth century and the nineteenth century—and sometimes even today—people have believed and still do believe this. I do not recall that Bronowski ever drew such a sharp and clear connection between the necessary *imperfection* of art and the necessary *incompleteness* of any scientific account of the world as the one I have drawn here, but it seems to me that he constantly implies it. I should add that I think that his philosophy is not only for the twentieth century, but also illuminating and helpful for this century and perhaps beyond, although, like any picture of the world, it is personal and limited, as he would have been the first to emphasise. Bronowski's ideas have, I believe, been unjustly neglected since his death and my motive in writing this book is to begin to redress that neglect.

Bronowski's philosophy is usually called scientific humanism, but handy labels are much less important than the description of what he believed about the world and in what important respects he differs from other philosophers. In trying to do this, I shall have a good deal to say about what he did *not* believe, and on what points he disagreed with other thinkers or flatly contradicted them. Every philosopher and everyone writing about philosophy must do this, and the method is as old as Socrates. To get an idea of what Bronowski is saying we have to turn aside at times and notice that he is nothing like Plato, nothing like Sartre and not much like Bertrand Russell. There are also some surprising resemblances, if only fleeting and limited ones. Further, comparing Bronowski with other thinkers and writers who lived before him, were contemporary with him or are still writing today carries out the vital task of putting him in some kind of context. This method used to be rather frowned on in some academic departments, although I have always found it difficult to understand why. Part of the enduring value of any writer's work, and an important part, is that it may at any time illuminate the world as a whole and help us to understand our own problems today, and so it is important to draw connections wherever possible. An interest in Roman history and Latin literature may well bring us to the relationship between Virgil and Augustus, and this may give us a sharper understanding of the relationship between Boris Pasternak and Stalin and of the issue of government power, literature and freedom of expression today. The more lines between similarities and dissimilarities we can draw, the more we clarify our understanding of the world as a whole. *Macbeth* may help us understand the life of Richard Nixon, and both may enrich our understanding of America in the last twenty years. 'We have to understand that the world can only be grasped by action, not by contemplation. The hand is more important than the eye...The hand is the cutting edge of the mind.' Bronowski said in *The Ascent of Man*, Chapter 3 — a statement that sets him sharply apart from a great many philosophers, both ancient and modern — and it is, of course, the statement of a professional scientist as well as a philosopher. There is an echo here of the famous declaration of Karl Marx, carved on his tombstone in Highgate Cemetery, from his *Theses on Feuerbach*: 'The philosophers have only *interpreted* the world, in various ways; the point, however, is to *change* it.' Marx came to believe that he was a scientist, analysing history and capitalist economy in a scientific manner, so that he proudly sent a copy of *Das Kapital* to Darwin after it was published. Surprisingly, the same point is made in vivid terms by a man who believed himself to be a Marxist, and who was a talented writer, however terrible the impact of his actions was upon the lives of millions of people — Mao Zedong: 'If you want knowledge, you must take part in the practice of changing reality. If you want to know the taste of a pear, you must change the pear by eating it yourself.' There the resemblance ends. Bronowski might well have said of The Great Leap Forward and The Cultural Revolution in Mao's China, as he said at Auschwitz: 'When people believe that they have absolute knowledge, with no test in reality, this is how they behave. This is what men do when they aspire to the knowledge of gods.'

Existentialism also stresses the importance of action and choice. Briefly, in the form that it is set out by Sartre, it stresses that human beings live in a godless and meaningless universe, set apart from the rest of the physical world by possessing will and consciousness. However, this condition is oppressive and it gives rise to *nausea* (a word that is the title of an early novel by Jean-Paul Sartre). Human beings can be free only by recognising that they can and should exercise choice and responsibility *alone* and without relying on some kind of external morality, but they usually make excuses to themselves — they act in *bad faith* — falling back on justifications from religion or bourgeois conceptions of laws and rights or upon rationalisations of their own weakness. This was an exciting and appealing philosophy that had great influence for several decades after the Second World War. Sartre was also a Marxist sympathiser, but he never quite managed to explain why anyone should freely choose to work for the revolution rather than freely choose to work against it. One of the sources of existentialism is the work of the late nineteenth century philosopher Friedrich Nietzsche who famously declared that: 'God is dead.' By this he meant that human society had advanced to the point at which religious belief was no longer credible and could not be taken seriously, and so there are no absolute truths or values. Therefore, like Sartre, he is inviting us to take the responsibility of embracing our own freedom, embracing human existence including its pain and choosing our own project in life. Nietzsche's Superman is an earlier version of Sartre's authentic, courageously aware, freely choosing individual. (There is a quite false notion, occasionally believed even today, that Nietzsche was a sort of proto-Nazi, and undoubtedly this notion was founded by Hitler himself, who was quite incapable of understanding Nietzsche's work. However, by picking up a few phrases, Hitler concluded that Nietzsche would have been in sympathy with his own vicious and mundane fantasies.) Bronowski was not an existentialist and did not have much sympathy for existentialism, and he explained why quite vividly.

Firstly, Bronowski regarded nature 'not as a constraint but an adventure', as he tells us in *The Identity of Man*, and of course he never lost sight of the fact that we are part of the natural, physical world. The imagination and ability to reason that make us unique on this planet did not give rise to any nausea in Bronowski; instead it created in him an excitement at the prospect of understanding the natural world of which we form a part and ourselves as a unique species. And he suggests that this should be the normal, appropriate response to life for all of us. Secondly, Nietzsche's Superman and Sartre's authentic, free individual are rather like the astronaut in the famous film *2001: A Space Odyssey*, who has broken his connection with the spaceship and goes tumbling off into space. (Bronowski did not use this illustration and I have invented it here in the hope of making a point vividly and concretely.) The point is that it is quite unrealistic simply to see ourselves as cut off, severed from the human past that has partly created us. We are members of the human species as well as individuals, and as such we are part of the human adventure and at a stage in the human journey of self-discovery, certainly able to make choices, but informed choices within that context. If we ignore what literature, physics, biology and history can tell us about the world and ourselves we will not make intelligent choices, and while our choices will still be free, the 'authentic' self we will create will turn out to be rather gratuitous and surprisingly uninteresting.

Philosophy, Sartre's included, is full of phrases such as 'Man brings nothingness into the world with him' or 'Man was born free, and he is everywhere in chains' or 'Man is a rope fastened between animal and Superman — a rope over an abyss' — all very stirring, and all implying that at any given point in time (or perhaps mysteriously outside time) there is some kind of abstract 'Man' or 'Human' who is always there but who is somehow unconnected with a million years of actual, concrete biological and cultural evolution. This way of thinking tends to suggest that we only have to define what form 'Man' or 'Human' takes in the abstract and then draw up rules for the way we live our lives. Even Marx, who is fairly free of this kind of abstraction, falls into it sometimes. And, of course, many philosophers are, in one way or another, telling us that they are bringing us the truth and that all philosophers before them were mistaken. However, the nearest approximation to the truth that we will ever have is a synthesis of all the knowledge accumulated through human history. Mathieu, the hero of Sartre's set of novels *The Roads to Freedom* is, by the end of the trilogy, fighting against the Nazi invasion of his country; but why would anyone fight against Hitler unless he/she had some kind of moral values partly instilled by the culture of the past? Bronowski insisted that there *are* values on which we can base our lives and our actions, and they come from the rigorous truthfulness and willingness to stick to the evidence of science, together with the sympathy and understanding that come from art, a different but no less important kind of knowledge. We desperately need both kinds of knowledge, and Bronowski is unusual among modern thinkers because he understood this so clearly and went on insisting upon it. Shakespeare makes us understand Macbeth, makes us somehow *sympathise* with him (a very different thing from 'agreeing' with Macbeth — no sane person can 'agree' with him), so that we are moved by Macbeth's fate more than we are moved by the fate of his victims, and we find him somehow more noble than those who quite justifiably destroy him. In sympathising with Macbeth we understand ourselves better, just as reading about the personal struggles of George Eliot's Dorothea Brooke or Doris Lessing's Anna Wulf will give us a sharper appreciation of our own difficulties and of the difficulties of the real people around us.

Above all, we need to be aware of ourselves as members of the human species, and we desperately need some grasp of where the human journey has so far brought us and of what needs to be done to go on to further achievements and make life more worth living on this planet, and of what needs to be avoided in order to escape a disastrous future. Without this awareness we cannot hope to understand wars in Afghanistan or Iraq — or future wars — and economic recession, or how we might provide for our fuel needs in the future, or the implications of genetic engineering or the renewed exploration of space. Very few people go through life without assessing the present and who they *are* by recalling their childhood and who they *were*. The human species has also had a long childhood — and perhaps the last two hundred years or so have been a noisy and destructive adolescence — and we may or may not go on to a long, productive adulthood that is worth living. If the human species is in its adolescence, then we must grasp that we are adolescents *together* on this planet. I quote the beautiful words of John Donne, a poet also admired and quoted by Bronowski, written four centuries ago.

> No man is an island, entire of itself; every man is a piece of the continent, a part of the main. If a clod be washed away by the sea, Europe is the less, as well as if a promontory were, as well as if a manor of thy friend's or of thine own were. Any man's death diminishes me, because I am involved in mankind; and therefore never send to know for whom the bell tolls; it tolls for thee (Meditation 17).

We might expect Bronowski's ideas to have much in common with the philosophy of Bertrand Russell (1872–1970), an English mathematician and philosopher who worked at Cambridge, but in fact the resemblance is not very great. Despite the success of his book *History of Western Philosophy* (1945), Russell lacked Bronowski's awareness of history and cultural evolution in the broader sense, and he lacked both the passion for science and the optimism that is so characteristic of Bronowski. It is not clear whether Russell considered the implications of quantum physics and the principle of uncertainty in relation to the point at which he had to abandon his own idea of mathematics as a continuation of logic dealing with essences outside both mind and matter. Bronowski, on the other hand, hailed the revolution in physics after the end of the 1920s and the revolution in biology after 1953 as the greatest achievements of the twentieth century. Further, he did not share Russell's dogmatic pacifism, because he knew that Hitler had to be defeated and that Nazi Germany might make the atomic bomb first: 'That was a race that no one who was loyal to the human tradition could afford to lose' (*Journey Round a Twentieth Century Skull*). Neither did he practise Russell's militant and rather tedious atheism, preferring to leave the question alone, and it should be added that there are some scientists writing today who would do well to do the same, instead of parading their atheism so dogmatically that they start to sound very much like the religious fundamentalists they clearly detest. Bronowski made occasional references to God, just as Einstein did, and it is hard to judge how literal or how metaphorical these were — he was, after all, a poet as well as a scientist.

\* \* \*

However, Bronowski's work makes no concessions to the objections of religious believers (and of some scientists with religious beliefs) when these are clearly mistaken and when they contradict a perfectly clear explanation of the evidence. One of these objections is as follows. Look at any living human being, you or me or anyone else. It is wildly, inconceivably unlikely that all the atoms in a human body, so the argument goes, would come together in one place and in one instant to make this wonderful creature, especially given what we know about the unpredictable behaviour of atomic particles, and so there must be some divine design at work in the universe to make this happen. If atoms did come together in such a way and make up a human being, then it would be almost impossible for even one human being to exist. But this is not what happens, because the whole wonderful process goes in stages.

> The atoms form molecules, the molecules form bases, the bases direct the formation of amino acids, the amino acids form proteins, and proteins work in cells. The cells make up first of all the simple animals, and then sophisticated ones, climbing step by step (*The Ascent of Man*).

Of course, disorderly states of matter are far more common than orderly states of matter and orderly states will usually run down into disorderly ones, but while this is probable, it does not always or inevitably happen, it is a statistical law, but not a law with certainty built into it. The exceptions to the probable trend allow orderly states to build up in certain areas of the universe — the stars, our own planet, our own bodies. Each of the stable units mentioned in Bronowski's explanation above — molecules, amino acids, cells, simple animals, complex animals — provide the setting and the opportunity for random encounters which produce higher configurations, a proportion of which will be stable. 'Evolution is the climbing of a ladder from simple to complex by steps, each of which is stable in itself.' Bronowski calls the process of evolution by which life on this planet has diversified into increasingly complex forms *Stratified Stability*.

### The Common Sense of Science (1951)

The main reason why many people who are non-scientists find it so difficult to take an interest in science in general is a lack of any kind of idea of the *history* of science, of a historical context. Bronowski rather touchingly compares this with his own difficulties at school when he first came to Britain, unable to read English easily until he was about fourteen or fifteen, and afterwards devouring English literature—Macaulay, Joseph Conrad, Dickens, Aphra Behn, Bernard Shaw, Marlowe, Coleridge, H. G. Wells—all greedily lumped together, but not accompanied by any knowledge of British history that might have enabled him to make sense of literary development. As I have argued above in summarising some of the basics of Bronowski's philosophy, we need some grasp of human evolution and history in order to understand the condition of human beings today, and similarly we need some grasp of the history of science in order to understand what science has done for us and what it can do for us. It is precisely this historical framework that he tries to provide in *The Common Sense of Science*.

When Bronowski wrote this book there was a widespread dislike of science on the grounds that it tends, in a scientific society, to marginalise the arts; and that dislike is still with us today. There is also the idea that while science and the technology it generates outgrow their old ideas and progress, great literature remains permanent. This was persuasively put forward in a scene in *The First Circle* by Alexander Solzhenitsyn (admittedly stunning for his courage as a dissident Russian writer, but also the darling of Western literary intellectuals and journalists for less admirable reasons in the 1960s and early 1970s).

'Progress!' Nerzhin snorted.

> Who wants progress? That's just what I like about art — the fact that there can't be any "progress" in it [...] in the seventeenth century there was Rembrandt, and he's still with us today, and nobody can improve on him, whereas seventeenth century technology now looks very crude to us. Or take the great inventions of the 1870s: we now think nothing at all of them, but has there been any advance on *Anna Karenina* which was written at the same time?

This is all very appealing but extremely muddled and mistaken. Bronowski points out that scientists of the stature of Newton and prose writers of the stature of Dryden are rare in any age and rare now. Similarly, to return to my own example above, writers like Tolstoy and scientists like Mendeleev (who carried out his work three or four years before *Anna Karenina* was published) are as rare today as they were in the late nineteenth century. Newton stands in the same relation to modern science Dryden stands in relation to modern prose, as Bronowski writes: 'Dryden and Newton each revealed a wholly new set of possibilities in their forms of knowledge.' To put it simply, without Dryden there would be no Orwell, Graham Greene or Doris Lessing, without Newton there would be no Einstein or Stephen Hawking, and without Tolstoy and Mendeleev there would be no Solzhenitsyn, no Sakharov or I.S. Shklovskii. Solzhenitsyn's sentimental traditionalism turns out to be as arbitrarily divorced from the past as Sartre's existentialism, and all the more surprising because Solzhenitsyn was trained as a mathematician and physicist, just as was his autobiographical hero Nerzhin.

In almost all the great ages of culture and achievement (the great flowering of the thirteenth century Icelandic prose sagas is an exception) science and art have flourished together, interpenetrating and complementing each other, and this is a demonstrable historical fact, at least from ancient Greece onwards. The notion of some kind of golden age in which art flourished without the harsh presence of cold science is an illusion. Bronowski also deals with the illusion that pre-industrial or non-industrial societies were or are less brutal than industrial and mechanised ones. As Orwell always insisted, before you can despise the machine, the machine has to set you free from brute labour. Pre-industrial societies lacked a certain sensibility, and although that seems a strange word to use today, it is an accurate one. Scottish miners were legally still serfs before the Industrial Revolution, women and children laboured in poor light for twelve hours a day in pre-industrial village cottages in conditions as terrible as in any 'satanic mill' or factory, and the fate of horses was infinitely worse before the combustion engine replaced them as the main means of land transport. Writers who lived before the Industrial Revolution saw nothing wrong in all this, and it was only the Romantic Age in literature and thought, following immediately from the Industrial Revolution, that created the sensibility that made educated individuals regard these things as horrors.

So far, so good. When people have looked back at the Middle Ages in the last two hundred years or so, however, they have either seen a legitimate and natural hierarchy and unity — reinforcing their own reactionary longings, often coupled with jolly peasant antics in a sort of continual spring day out of Chaucer's *Canterbury Tales* (writers as widely divergent in tendency and seriousness as William Morris, W.B. Yeats, T.S. Eliot, G.K. Chesterton, Alexander Solzhenitsyn and J.R.R. Tolkien have indulged in this attitude, and one of their present gifted apologists is Solzhenitsyn's biographer Joseph Pearce) — or they have seen dirt, lice, heretics burnt at the stake and ignorance. There is some truth in both views, but neither is particularly helpful. There *was* great learning and there *was* intellectual enquiry in the medieval world — within limits set by the authority of the Church — and medieval thinkers were not ignorant or irrational, in fact they were just as rational as any scientist or philosopher today. Medieval Christianity, much influenced by Aristotle, was profound enough to order things into permanent classes according to the fact that they had a likeness to each other but were not identical, such as, for instance, apples—the very things that fall downwards from a tree and set Newton thinking—and this was a considerable leap in human thought. The point at which medieval thinking diverges from our own conception of the world since Newton is the notion that apples fall from trees because it is the nature of that class of things to fall downwards. For Aristotle and for medieval minds, all things were either earth, water, air or fire, or combinations of those elements, and these elements possessed a certain nature of their own, a certain will of their own. In this respect the thought of the Middle Ages has similarities with many other societies that anthropomorphise the physical world, endowing it with human-like qualities. There are virtues in this outlook, and the outlook itself has been renewed and embraced by certain movements in our own society today, that often quote with sympathy, the fate of the Native Americans who held onto the belief that all things are sacred and alive while being driven from their homes and exterminated by Europeans. We need to recognise, however, that if this belief system had persisted in Europe, together with the social structure that went with it, each of them supporting the other, then the most basic, indispensable conditions for what we see as a tolerable existence for the overwhelming majority of human beings would never have materialised. The thinkers of the Middle Ages could not conceive of the natural world as being *mechanical*, instead of being driven on by the nature or will of its elements, but of course nature is mechanical; yet many people today recoil from that description for quite mistaken reasons. This is a point of crucial importance that I shall return to a little further on. Medieval thought proceeded from this starting point, and given the starting point, the thinking was perfectly rational.

The hierarchical world of the Middle Ages—with its pyramid-like feudal structure, from monarch down to privileged aristocracy to warrior knights to peasants, all fixed in their social class, with people bound generation after generation to their craft or social position—disintegrated slowly from the late fifteenth century through the sixteenth century and on into the seventeenth century, gradually giving way to a society more dominated by merchants, by trade and industry and profit. In the seventeenth century the tempo of change accelerated, and in England specifically the outer political and religious forms of change were Puritanism and Cromwell's revolution. As the social structure changed, the older ideas weakened and new, dynamic concepts jostled in to replace them, so changing the social structure further and opening the way for still more original ideas. In England the political issues were settled first. The Civil War and Cromwell's revolution permanently altered the power relationship between parliament, representing the rising merchant class and the non-aristocratic sections of society on the one hand, and on the other hand, the monarchy and the feudal aristocracy. Cromwell's long dictatorship was not tolerant, but it broke the hold of medieval, feudal power forever. The Restoration in 1660, the recall of Charles II to be king of England, happened without further war and violence because the economic and political struggle had been settled. All this paved the way for the Scientific Revolution of the seventeenth century, which could only have happened in a culture more liberal than anything that had gone before, and of course, this great revolution was a phenomenon that extended across all of Europe. Bronowski is surely right in seeing the founding of the Royal Society of London for Improving Natural Knowledge (now known as simply the Royal Society) as the collective expression of this great shift in human thinking. Charles II could not have had much affection for the leading scientists and scholars of the Royal Society, most of whom were Puritans or held Puritan sympathies or had been actually promoted by Cromwell, but he gave his approval and the title 'royal' to the organisation. The founding of the Royal Society was mirrored by the foundation of the Royal Academy in France in 1666. In the 1660s, more than a century before the French social and political revolution, Louis XIV 'acquiesced in a universal change of outlook', as Bronowski put it. This profound change of outlook permeated all Europe and underlay both politics and science, creating a momentum that made it possible for Christian Huygens, a Dutchman, a Protestant and a Cartesian to be summoned to France to help found the Royal Academy. Bronowski was later to describe science as 'less brittle than the rage of tyrants' when he wrote of French scientists defying Napoleon in awarding a prize to Humphry Davy in 1807.

Similarly, if one individual can be said to embody a great historical revolution in his/her lifetime, then Isaac Newton embodied the Scientific Revolution in his life, his work, his thought and his actions, and Bronowski is quite correct to emphasise this point. More than any other individual who lived after him Newton reshaped our world because the implications of his thought permeate everything. Newton's work made possible the technology and infrastructure of life that you and I and the whole world now take for granted. It is largely because of Newton that a person like myself can write this book and you are able to read it. It is because of the consequences of Newton's work that a man like Bronowski became a scientist and wrote his own books and so became an influence upon the world worth remembering.

\* \* \*

Bronowski emphasises that Newton, like all scientists, had a style of his own, something that he kept emphasising with regard to science, and I have already touched on this point above and will do so again. Engagingly, he refers to 'the whole of Newton, the man and the manner, the large nose and the strong thumbprint of his style'. This question of personal style, of the creativity and imagination in science, is absolutely vital to understanding what science is and how it is done. It is still widely believed even today that scientists carry out observations or experiments, and having piled up results upon results they then conclude that there are scientific laws at work in the universe. This is not how scientific laws are formulated, least of all by great minds like Newton's. Newton, like Einstein, began with an *idea*, with a picture or model of how the universe works, and indeed, that is all that science is — a model or a picture, and just as Newton's picture, or classical Newtonian physics, as it is called, was eventually replaced by a better picture that included and explained more, by Einstein's Relativity physics and by quantum physics and Heisenberg's principle of uncertainty, so Relativity and quantum physics are in process of being replaced by other, and better, models or pictures. Certainly, the model or picture must be tested and tested again against the known facts and against the observable evidence, and if it fits the facts and the evidence the scientist will become more confident that the picture is right, and the picture will become sharper, clearer, suggesting more observations and experiments to test its validity.

> Science does not consist only of finding the facts; nor is it enough only to think, however rationally. The processes of science are characteristic of human action in that they move by the union of empirical fact and rational thought, in a way which cannot be disentangled. There is in science, as in all our lives, a continuous to and fro of actual discovery, then of thought about the implications of what we have discovered, and so back to the facts for testing and discovery — a step by step of experiment and theory, left, right, left, right, forever.

Bronowski writes in *The Common Sense of Science* in his chapter on Isaac Newton. We can, therefore, think of a great scientific theory as similar to a great work of art. *Hamlet* or *Middlemarch* or a Beethoven symphony or a Rembrandt painting surely all began with the exciting embryo of an idea, but the creative artist still had to patiently write and rewrite, make drafts and perhaps discard them, in order to arrive at something worth watching on the stage, worth reading on the page, worth listening to or looking at on the canvas, something that holds together as an artistic whole and moves us emotionally and sets us thinking. Bronowski did not, to my knowledge, draw quite such an exact analogy between science and artistic creation, but the analogy seems to me to be a good one, as well as being — once again — implied in everything that he did write. The fact that science evolves and progresses does not discredit science, as some people seem to think, any more than literature is discredited because writers have dared to go on writing novels since *Middlemarch* was published, but the kind of novels that have been written since George Eliot would not have been written if she had never lived. Empirical testing and logical thinking are, therefore, insufficient on their own and indeed are meaningless if they are separated from each other, and the roots of the Scientific Revolution lie in the realisation of Galileo and his contemporaries that the two methods have to be put together — although, of course, other roots stretch still further back in history, and Bronowski warns us not to think of single, dramatic, abrupt turning points in history in the way that the philosopher A.N. Whitehead describes them. Both the rather abstract logic of Descartes, who nonetheless grasped that there is a single, mathematical unity in all of nature, and the robust practical experiments of his English contemporary Francis Bacon were a powerful influence on Newton.

\* \* \*

Newton was born during Cromwell's revolution and reached the age of eighteen at the time of the Restoration in 1660, and so he lived at a time of great instability and change in European history. There were, so to speak, vast historical upheavals shaking the very ground under his feet, and yet periods of change and upheaval are extremely fertile for profound thinking, just as — to extend my metaphor — volcanic ash can later provide a rich fertiliser for the earth. Newton did not, of course, create or cause these upheavals, but they were a great stimulus for his work, which in turn focussed and reflected the historical changes in the form of a great scientific theory. I would suggest that profound minds intuitively sense the ferment of the times, and that it is no coincidence that a great novelist like Joseph Conrad, breaking with the old idea of a single 'reality' conveyed by an omniscient author, and a great scientist like Einstein, breaking with the older concept of a universal 'now', were doing their best work at the same time, in the years immedi-

ately before 1914, the cataclysm that smashed the old order
and the old certainties.

Galileo and others had been groping towards a consistent
model of how the world works, but it was Newton who tri-
umphantly provided it. He began with a picture of the
world in which everything is assembled of small particles
(he never strictly defined these particles as atoms), and yet
he pictured the pebble, the apple, the Moon, the sun and the
planets as assemblies of these particles, and he believed that
in everything the particles obey the same laws. If the particles are still, they remain still until some force moves them,
and if they are moving they go on moving until some force
stops them. The greatest and the universal force is that of
gravitation, the force that attracts every particle to every
other particle and every big assembly of particles to every
other big assembly, and it is a force that gets weaker *at a definite, measurable rate* as the distance between particles and
assemblies of particles grows larger. Certain definite consequences and propositions logically flow from Newton's
picture—that large, spherical assemblies of particles like
the Sun and the planets pull other bodies outside that
sphere towards a point at the centre of the sphere. Newton
then went on to do the mathematics, to make the calculations of the consequences of his picture of the universe, and
the calculations fitted what manifestly could be seen to happen, so that he *was* able to calculate the orbits of the planets,
the tides and the paths of comets, so that his speculations
were 'suddenly seen to chime with the real world, with a tri-
umphant note like a peal of bells' as Bronowski describes it.
Newton did not make experiment after experiment and
deduce his laws from them, but instead he came up with a
picture of how the universe works that predicted how
things will happen, and the way in which things happen
confirmed that his predictions were right. The very same
laws and the very same force that make the apple fall from
the tree to the ground also keep the Moon in its orbit around
the Earth and the Earth in its orbit around the Sun. And
when Dylan Thomas wrote his beautiful lines:

> The force that through the green fuse drives the flower
> Drives my green age; that blasts the roots of trees
> Is my destroyer

he was saying much the same thing, showing us the same world that Newton revealed through his model and his mathematics.

Newton's picture of the universe gave the idea of cause and effect, of *causality*, a powerful and compelling new form, although the idea of cause and effect is a common sense idea, not unique to science. The picture also endured for more than two hundred years — the mathematics and physics were superb, we can make jet airliners fly based on them. It was left to Einstein, Heisenberg, Relativity and quantum physics to demonstrate the flaw in Newton's great picture: namely that he saw time and space as absolute, the same for all observers, implying that there is in the universe a strict sequence of causes and effects, with each effect following from a cause that precedes it, so that if we can only know enough about the present we can map and predict the future with certainty. This is an extension of common sense, but while, in Bronowski's words the world 'makes common sense', we cannot quite describe it in commonsensical terms if we insist that strict steps of cause and effect are essential to common sense.

Strangely, after the wonderful heights of the Scientific Revolution of the seventeenth century, science was on the decline in the eighteenth century, and the beginnings of the antipathy between scientists and artists go back to this decline, and to this period can be traced the 'two cultures', the phrase coined by the writer C.P. Snow in 1959 to describe the situation in which scientific intellectuals and literary intellectuals fail to be able to communicate with each other in modern society. There was a sour debate between Snow and the literary critic F.R. Leavis conducted through lectures in the early sixties that has now passed into academic legend, although the phrase is still frequently used and the situation it describes is still with us. Sadly, Snow and Leavis and their followers had more influence and notoriety in this area than Bronowski's sane and 'common sense' insistence that science and art are inseparable and can—and should—flourish together. In my own lifetime I have known people with great taste in literature and great knowledge of it combined with a fastidious contempt for scientists and a pride in their ignorance of basic scientific ideas. Poets and satirists like Swift and Pope and Gay were defeated and embittered Tories and the scientists of the Royal Society were frequently Whigs and dissenters, so that the rivalry had social and political roots, but as the eighteenth century unfolded the writers and intellectuals of the Whig party also became unsympathetic to scientists and the Royal Society became a club for gentlemen in which scientists were 'a cowed and servile minority' as Bronowski describes them. It was also in the eighteenth century that England became a manufacturing nation, so that the practical science that was done was carried out by frequently self-taught engineers and specialists at home in the world of coal and iron and wool and brilliant in their fields of experiment and invention. Their social origins excluded them from the Royal Society where they might have interacted with and informed the mathematicians interested in filling out the picture of how the world works. Instead, lively intellectual life seems to have moved away to smaller learned societies well outside London, in northern England and the Midlands. The majestic quality of Newton's model of the universe also became damaging because it was so all encompassing, creating the impression that there was nothing else to discover and hardening into a dogma that delayed further scientific progress, a dogma that asserted that there was a single mathematical system that described nature and that it could be calculated precisely. This conviction or dogma continued late into the nineteenth century and became the obsession of Victorian science. It was finally overthrown in the first decades of the twentieth century, something that brings us to the heart of science and of what science is telling us about the world.

There is nothing wrong in describing the processes of nature observed by science as machines, for they are precisely that, although a widespread misunderstanding makes many people—even today—view this description with horror, scepticism or contempt. Bronowski explains: 'A machine in science is a concept with definite properties which can be isolated, can be reproduced in space and time, and whose behaviour can be predicted.' Therefore, if the required material conditions are present we can predict the result—a light comes on when we press a switch and a child learns to speak as she/he grows older. If the light does not come on when we press the switch or the child does not learn to speak, then clearly one of the conditions is missing or an extra condition has been introduced into the situation. So far, none of this is hard to grasp—nature and the physical world are *mechanical*. This description becomes oppressive to many people because it is confused with the concept of cause and effect, a concept—as we have seen—that was given enormously more force and clarity by the Scientific Revolution and by Isaac Newton especially. Two hundred years later, in the nineteenth century, the calculation of cause and effect became *the* scientific method, and to the Victorians it *was* science. It was a concept that took science, as a description or picture of the world, an enormous distance, but it could only take science so far.

Hence the discoveries of quantum physics, begun by Max Planck in 1900 and finally formulated by Heisenberg in 1927 as the principle of uncertainty, overthrew this concept. The position of an electron can be measured with some accuracy, but the more accurately we measure its position, the less certain we become of its speed, and the more precisely we measure its speed, the more uncertain we become of its position. We cannot, in fact, predict the future of a particle with certainty because we cannot be certain of its present state, and the particles do not move and behave tidily according to Newton's laws of cause and effect. Also, particles are not always particles because they are sometimes waves and behave as waves. Newton's wonderful picture of the universe was being replaced by a better, sharper picture of reality that included more, but it was not a picture containing more and more precise calculations—quite the opposite. Quantum physics showed that an amount of uncertainty is built into any description of nature. Further, the electrons in the atoms that make up the large molecules in our brains and nerves and our genes all behave in this uncertain way.

Einstein had demonstrated that we cannot measure the time in one place against the time in another place without sending information, and this information will take time to pass between two points, so that there is no universal 'now', but only a 'here and now' for each observer in each place. If the Sun ceased to exist and give out light in an instant, it would continue to shine in our sky for several minutes because light waves would take those minutes to travel to Earth and those light waves already on their way would keep coming, from our point of view, well after the Sun ceased to exist. The Sun's 'now', the moment in which it ceased to exist, would not be the same 'now' as ours here on Earth when we would become aware that it had stopped shining. Similarly, if you go out at night and look at a star twenty-five light years away, you are not looking at the star as it is in the star's present, you are looking at it as it was twenty-five years ago in the star's past. The concept of cause and effect and of the present completely determining the future is not, therefore, the true and self-evident description of reality that it was once taken to be. We can predict proba- ble outcomes but we must allow for what Bronowski describes as 'some uncertainty: some range of alternatives, some slack — what engineers call some tolerance'. It was the conviction of the French astronomer and mathematician Pierre Simon de Laplace (1749–1827) that if we knew with complete accuracy the position and speed of every particle of matter in the universe in the present, then we could pre- dict the future precisely and for all eternity. Bronowski reminds us:

> he believed that in principle it could be done, if not by a human then by a superhuman computer. He believed that the future is fully and finally determined. The future as it were already exists in the mathematics.

However, we can never know what the present *is* with cer- tainty and so we cannot predict the future with certainty.

Can we still validly believe that the future is determined, even though it is impossible to predict? Bronowski's reply is humorous and laced with exasperation.

> This is an attractive suggestion, but I think rather pathetic; because what it really says is that if the questioner has to choose between science and causality, then he prefers to plump for causality [...] To try to make a nice distinction between what science can predict and what is somehow supernaturally determined is a piece of elegant but really quite shameless self-deception. Science is a practical study of what can be observed, and the prediction from that of what will be observed. To say that causes are somehow getting under this observable world, when anything under it is essentially unobservable, is neither helpful nor meaningful; it is just a piece of faithful comfort. We might as well say that electrons are really pushed about by blue fairies with red noses [...] If they are essentially unobservable, beyond all hope of future unravelling, then it simply does not make sense to bring them into any system, logical, metaphysical, or even religious.

The probable future can usually be predicted with considerable confidence, but it is no more than probability, and no scientific laws or methods exist that can overcome this difficulty. Yes, the world is mechanical — lights will come on when we press the switch and children will learn to speak as they grow older, given the necessary set of conditions, but we can never know with certainty if or when some new condition will be introduced into the situation or if or when some essential condition will be removed so that the outcome will change. The same is true of our brains, our genes, our actions and our reactions. In the shifting, dynamic picture of the world that quantum physics gives us the future is not fixed. The implications of this reached out into the dry, tight world of logic and geometry in the first half of the twentieth century. It came to be realised that perfectly sensible questions could be asked that led to propositions and theorems being formulated that could not be shown to be either true or false.

As we watch a film or a play or read a novel we ask ourselves: what will the characters do next? As we live our lives we ask ourselves: what will happen tomorrow and what will I do? We will never *know* in advance, but only after we have lived through tomorrow or come to the end of the film, drama or novel. Far from insisting on some kind of clanking, reductionist, predictable clockwork in the present and the future and inside our own minds and bodies, it is the great achievement of science in the last hundred years to confirm, compellingly and convincingly, the uncertainty and excitement that we feel in our own lives and in literature and art.

\*   \*   \*

If uncertainty is built into the world, then surely chance must play a part, as indeed it does. To many of us this seems a depressing conclusion—after all, science is supposed to make definite discoveries about the world and to come up with laws. We may say: How can we be sure that the sun will rise tomorrow? Perhaps by some chance it will not. Or: I am perfectly healthy, but perhaps by some chance I will stop breathing tonight, mysteriously, not because of any illness or accident. Where, then, have all the scientific laws gone? The answer is that we have scientific laws, but they are statistical laws, rather than laws with 'certain' and 'always' built into them. But at the mention of the word 'statistical' the eyes of many people glaze over with boredom or narrow with suspicion. Again and again on our television screens the latest 'expert' or politician or advertiser will say: 'Statistics clearly show that…' We switch channels muttering: 'You can prove anything by statistics.' However, the problem here is that 'experts' and politicians and advertisers select the statistics that suit them and conceal the rest from us, or that they base their statistics on such a small group that the results have no scientific standing or validity at all. Some years ago I listened to a radio programme in which a health worker declared: 'Someone is infected with HIV in Wales every six hours.' It sounded terrifying until I began to think about what it really meant. It meant that there were 1,460 new cases of HIV in Wales per year at that time (assuming that the health worker's original figures were correct) in a country of 2,800,000, or 2.8 million, people. The health worker, whose intentions were good ones, meaning to warn people of risks, had divided the figure of 1,460 by the number of days in a year—365 days, and come up with the figure of four new cases of HIV per day, and as every day lasts twenty-four hours, he concluded that someone was infected every six hours. He didn't make any distinction between persons who were infected by injecting drugs or by medical negligence, and he didn't make any distinction between people on the basis of their gender, lifestyle or sexual preference, and he certainly didn't look at other factors that might have shown that the rate of infection was speeding up or slowing down. Finally, of course, common sense tells us that the spread of HIV would not take place neatly at the rate of one case every six hours, but that new infections would be grouped around occasions when individuals tend to have sex on impulse when their inhibitions are lowered—a Friday or Saturday night perhaps—and so some age groups might be at more risk than others.

The intentions of the health worker I recall were good, but this can hardly be said of the politician who wants to be voted in again or the advertiser who wants to sell more of a particular brand of shampoo or cat food or the editor who wants to sell more copies of his or her newspaper. As we have already noticed, the formulation of a scientific law almost always begins with an imaginative leap, but then it has to be tested again and again against the known evidence and the observable facts. A statistical law in science is still a law despite the fact that it doesn't contain the words 'certain' and 'always'—as long as it is tested rigorously. This scientific, rigorous quality is precisely what 'statistics' as understood by the cabinet minister and the cat food manufacturer lack. The scientists who find statistical laws in nature should not be blamed for the antics of present day politicians, journalists and advertisers any more than scientists through history should be blamed for extravagant frauds, quacks, or indeed for leaders like Hitler, who also regarded his ignorant and vicious notions to have been proved by statistics. Bronowski himself considers a number of concrete situations to which the statistical method has been or might be applied, including his own observation that Americans of European origin were usually taller than Japanese Americans and Japanese Americans were usually taller than the Japanese from Japan itself, as well as the effect of streptomycin on tuberculosis and of smoking on lung cancer.

I will offer here, however, a simple example of my own that may make the way in which statistical laws are formulated clearer, because the example itself is more impersonal and so, perhaps, more accessible. Supposing that there is a fairly rare condition, Disease X, which is developed by 0.5 % (half of one per cent) of the population every year over a period of many years during which good records have been kept. Then we notice that out of a group of ten people whose work has brought them into close contact with Substance Y, eight are suffering from Disease X. Well, we may say, that is just coincidence, or these people are just unlucky. And that would be the right response if we stopped at just ten people. However, if we test a hundred people and then a thousand people and then a hundred thousand people who have worked with Substance Y, and we find that eight out of ten of them, or 80% are suffering from Disease X, then we have established a statistical law of probability: prolonged contact with Substance Y greatly increases the chances of developing Disease X, and we don't have to say just 'greatly increases' because we can put a figure on the probability. There will, of course, always be the unfortunate 0.5 % of people who have never come into contact with Substance Y but still develop Disease X, and there will be the lucky 20 % who have worked with the substance for years and never developed the disease — this is the area of uncertainty. And yet the margin of uncertainty can be calculated, measured, just as the probability can be calculated, and this is just as much a scientific law as any law that tells us what will certainly happen.

\* \* \*

In human terms, no one can be sure that they will be one of the 80% who work with the substance and get the disease or one of the 20% in close contact with it who do not get the condition. In social terms, perhaps Substance Y should be banned by law (as real life substances have been banned). Those who make a great deal of money from the use of Substance Y will probably do their best to discredit the findings, drawing a great deal of attention to those who have worked with it for years and never contracted the disease. We have to consider other factors, of course, for instance, are the overwhelming majority of the hundred thousand people we test women over forty? If so, could the reason for developing Disease X be something to do with diet, or a genetic factor? But if we go on testing and find that no such factor is present, then we have tested the statistical law of probability to the limit of what can be scientifically tested. I believe, just as Bronowski believed, that scientific knowledge—in this instance a basic grasp of how laws of statistical probability are formed—could have an explosive effect on society if most people were familiar with that knowledge, just as a proper teaching of history would be explosive. The newspapers and television stuff all our heads with partial statistics, or with statistics that are unreliable because they are based on too small a group; but if most people understood, with no illusions, that *full statistics* are indeed to be found with enough effort, then perhaps we would all be less easy to manipulate by those who have a vested interest in manipulating us.

> "Publish and be damned." The human race will only learn how to use knowledge well by having knowledge disclosed to it, and the choice thrust down its throat (*Journey Round a Twentieth Century Skull*).

The chapter that follows the one on the concept of chance, 'The Common Sense of Science', bearing the same title as the book as a whole, is not, in my opinion, on the same level as the chapters that precede it. Some passages are rather obscure by Bronowski's standards, lacking his usual lucidity, and he also seems to dwell too long on the kind of philosophy from which he wanted to escape. Still, the chapter begins well with a passionate restatement of the awareness that Relativity and quantum physics have—or should have—brought us, both within science and within philosophy. Newton's model or picture of the world (we might say his philosophy of the world) was a good enough working approximation, and with it human beings were able to make steam engines work and fly planes and solve a great many mathematical problems. But as a guide to exploring reality, it only stood up so far and no further because it described the universe as a 'network of events', a strict sequence of causes and effects—in fact, it implied that the events of the physical world are there for us to observe as spectators in a detached way. However, in order to know about an event we have to receive information about it, a light wave from the sun or a star or the light waves we direct at a particle, and this information will not only take time to travel to us (or may affect the behaviour of the particle), it is part of the event we are observing and of the universe as a whole:

> Event, signal, and observer: that is the relationship which Einstein saw as the fundamental unit in physics. Relativity is the understanding of the world not as events but relations.

So insists Bronowski, and indeed we cannot get away from this reality, because, as he adds: 'all science [...] is active. It does not watch the world, it tackles it.' This is a radical break with much of philosophy throughout history. The world cannot be understood by simply thinking about it, however profoundly, as was believed in the Middle Ages, and it cannot be understood as something out there, quite separate from us, even by rational thinking and painstaking experiment combined, as Galileo and Newton believed, because by observing the world you put something of yourself into it, you affect it, and you are part of the world you are observing.

It is important to say something briefly about a dreadful development in the study of history and other subjects in recent years that seems to be loosely connected with this insight, a development that has been wittily exposed by Eric

Hobsbawm, who is, like Bronowski, someone who came to Britain from Europe at a young age. If we must put something of ourselves into every observation or interpretation of the world, the argument goes, and if we all do this, then any firmly held belief about the world is as 'historical' and 'accurate' as any other (including perhaps Hitler's?). This in no way follows, and we can see more clearly than ever why Bronowski insisted that the rigorous testing against observable fact and sticking to the evidence that are part of science are also part of any moral philosophy. Although we can never arrive at clear cut certainty about the world as something separate from ourselves, that does not mean that any account of the world is as 'true' as any other. We can, through effort and the pursuit of truth, arrive at an account of the world that is *as close to certainty as possible*.

Bronowski emphasises, and perhaps overemphasises, the fact that human action, including science, is future-directed, directed towards some future goal, and that this is true of all living things. Action and living are the same, and individual living things and whole species of animals can only survive if they interpret the signals given by the present to adapt to the future. I am writing this page today with the intention of finishing the whole book shortly, and the fox slips through the streets and fields at dusk with the intention of grabbing a readily available supper, and the movements of the simplest cell are also directed towards some future state; and this holds true whether actions are instinctive and unconscious and whether, as human beings, we believe our actions to be 'free' or not. We all have our private predictions of the future, but science deals in collective, general and explicit predictions or forecasts; not the *certain* ones that Laplace thought we could make if only we had enough information — because certain predictions would mean that the future already exists — but instead probable, statistical predictions.

For over two centuries philosophers have made the distinction between *deductive* reasoning and *inductive* reasoning that looks at the past and projects the lessons of the past into the future. There isn't much in this distinction in my view, and labouring away at making the distinction is one of the driest and least rewarding aspects of philosophy. As Bronowski clearly thought the same, he seems to me to give too much space to considering it, but he writes with his usual brio.

> But this distinction is much overrated. All that can be said about deduction is that we can state its processes, and give rules for deciding what is acceptable, in a precise form. But the sanctions for believing that its conclusions will be true tomorrow because they were true yesterday are no different from those which apply to any other theory which claims to reach into the future. If a triangle has three equal sides, then its three angles will be equal, we say. But what we mean is still that the three angles *are* equal; we have deduced that they are so by steps of logic which have always yielded sound results. If we say that the three angles will be equal, then we claim that these steps will continue to be allowable and will yield true results in the future. And this claim is typically an induction from the past to the future.

When we see that the strict sequence of cause and effect isn't really there in the world and that uncertainty is built into the world, we also see that some predictions will turn out to be wrong, or partly wrong. If the predictions of scientists turn out to be wrong, then this often arouses resentment in non-scientists, perhaps because we are still craving for the old laws with 'always' and 'definitely' built into them. But perhaps we should extend to science one of the basic truths of our own lives — that mistakes are productive, they are part of the learning process that is essential to human beings and to all animals. J.K. Rowling, the creator of the Harry Potter novels, once remarked: 'Almost all mistakes, apart from those involving a loaded gun, are beneficial in one way or another.' How right she was! Science is a self-correcting process of learning throughout history, from Galileo to Newton to Einstein and Heisenberg. If we are tempted to reply that Hiroshima and Nagasaki were not mistakes that could be corrected, and that for the thousands who died in those places the mistakes were of the 'loaded gun' variety, let us remember that Szilard and the leading scientists who had worked on the atomic bomb campaigned against its use against Japan. This mistake, like others, was one made by politicians. As for philosophy, Bronowski says that philosophers 'put the cart before the horse when they say that science constructs a world by sorting out what the experiences of different people have in common.' Science looks for the world that underlies our individual experiences and for the laws at work in that world, and it has to be explicit about those laws, making them as precise as possible because the laws have to be communicated to the rest of society, whereas you and I need not describe our personal experiences or our personal predictions. We do not analyse our day to day experiences in terms of 'cells and co-enzymes and mesons and genes and curved space', but he goes on rather curtly: '[The philosophies] of Berkeley and Hume and McTaggart and Moore [...] all start from a point inside the head of one person.' For myself, I would add that they then often generalise from that point inside one human head to the abstract 'Man' or 'Human' that I referred to earlier when discussing Sartre and Nietzsche. Bronowski did not, of course, ignore the value of describing unique personal experience—literature does this all the time—and he was unusual among scientists for his insistence that literature gives us a knowledge every bit as valid and valuable as the knowledge that comes from science. But it is a *different kind* of knowledge. It is the mistake of some philosophers to try to describe the general, impersonal shape of the world by starting from personal experience, or, to put it more crudely, some philosophers start from personal experience and then stray into the territory of science.

At the end of the chapter Bronowski gives another reason for the fact that our actions and the actions of all living things are future-directed. In the picture of the universe that has replaced Newtonian physics only one thing gives time a direction—the second law of thermodynamics that states that entropy always increases in any closed system that is not in equilibrium. Put simply, this means that matter in the universe is always running down into a more and more disorderly state, with the molecules and the atoms that make up the matter moving in a more and more random manner.

The matter that makes up human beings and other living things, however, is always moving into a more and more orderly state, and we could not survive if it was not. Bronowski claims that living things, and human beings especially, are 'attuned' to the more random or disorderly quality of the future, that we sense it and direct our actions to impose order upon the future. He does not, however, expand upon this interesting point any further.

In the following chapter Bronowski dismisses the philosophy of logical positivism, then at the peak of its influence, in a lively way. That philosophy, which we still hear echoed today, claims that the only true statements that it is possible to make about the world are statements that can be checked or verified against the facts, such as 'water is made up of hydrogen and oxygen'. Statements about right and wrong, about how we ought to act, about ethics and morality, are all comforting but strictly meaningless, the logical positivists claimed, because they cannot be verified. The philosophy originated in Vienna in the 1920s and later evolved into logical empiricism in America. Further, the logical positivists asserted that knowledge must be built up of sequences of factual statements following from each other. This is not how our minds work, and it is not how we have made discoveries about the world. To offer an example of my own: I do not recognise my wife when I see her by going through a mental checklist (however rapidly) of the colour of her hair, the colour of her eyes, her height, the shape of her face and so on. This is not how my daughter recognised me, even when she was a very young child, and it is not how my dog recognises me now. Our minds deal in huge complexes of these sense experiences, in 'integrated bundles' of sense experiences as Bronowski calls them. The logical positivists do seem to be defending science, or a certain notion of science, which is why we still hear their claims being quoted even today, sadly, sometimes by scientists, and sometimes by those hostile to science, even if they have barely heard of logical positivism. But this philosophy is rooted in nineteenth century science, in the conviction that beneath our experiences is a world of facts that can be *measured and pre-*

*dicted exactly*. A simple statement such as 'this is red' runs into the difficulties that were understood after the coming of Relativity and quantum physics. 'This' as a precise point in space and time cannot be measured exactly and 'red' is part of the spectrum of light with a definite wavelength, but that wavelength can only be measured with a margin of error, a degree of uncertainty. There is also the extraordinary fact — discussed by Bronowski in his later work — that our eyes do not passively transmit a signal that is received by our brains, but instead they begin to select and arrange information before it reaches our brains. We cannot judge what is true by making simple statements of fact and then verifying them beyond doubt, because, in Bronowski's words, 'the facts do not keep still for us, either in space or time'. For clarity, and especially in view of certain fashionable intellectual trends in recent years, I would repeat that an amount of necessary uncertainty does *not* mean that the statement 'the Earth is flat' is as true as any other, because unlike the description of the Earth as a rotating spherical body orbiting the sun, 'the Earth is flat' is a statement that completely fails to explain thousands of pieces of evidence, and no useful laws can be derived from it.

There were some scientists even in the nineteenth century who foresaw the necessary uncertainty in the world, and Bronowski quotes William Clifford (1845–79) for whom he clearly feels enormous admiration, 'the truth at which [science] arrives is not that which we can ideally contemplate without error, but that which we may act upon without fear'. Not all predictions are accurate, but science is not only a matter of facts and predictions, but rather reaches forward to find general laws, and these laws are still helpful and instructive although they tell us what will probably happen, not what will certainly happen. Science is not only a description of a huge accumulation of facts, it searches for an order within the facts, an order within the universe, an order made up of scientific laws that fit together coherently like the words of a poem (and, of course, we cannot precisely define the meaning of any word with complete certainty, but this does not prevent the poem making sense, having an overall coherence). It is here that the insistence of the logical positivists that the only meaningful statements we can make are ones we can verify beyond doubt, and that all knowledge is made up of such statements, can be seen to break down and become obviously mistaken. We can act 'without fear' upon scientific laws, not because they are basic statements that can never be disproved, but because they fit together coherently and make sense.

The account of science and truth that the logical positivists wanted to give is very much tied up with the notion — believed in several decades ago and sometimes also today — that there is no morality in science, no right and wrong, no values. However, science certainly contains the values of truthfulness and faithfulness to the evidence, and it could not exist without these values. Furthermore, science does in fact create, promote and generate moral values, because as a force in history and a force that helps to shape history, science creates a new *sensibility* by its discoveries. By searching for order within the world and within the facts, science establishes what is like and unlike, and this is a radical, fundamental step in human thought. In Ancient Greece slavery was not considered wrong because the slave and the citizen were not considered to be alike. Today, the *fact* of slavery still exists in some countries, but instead of openly defending it, people conceal it and call it by other names, whereas the *idea* of slavery has been killed in the world and it has been killed partly by science. By the end of the eighteenth century all White Europeans were thought to be alike, but men like William Wilberforce acted upon the new sensibility and spent their lives convincing society that White Europeans and Black slaves were alike and deserved the same human dignity. Later generations convinced society that women and men are alike and deserve the same respect and the same rights. Sensibility was widened by science so that other animals came to be seen as sufficiently like human beings to make cruelty to them a criminal offence.

\* \* \*

Science has certainly put new and more horribly efficient ways of killing and waging war into the hands of politicians, but it has also created the technical means of prolonging life and making it enormously more bearable for the human race, sometimes (though not nearly often enough) for members of the poorest societies on the planet, and it is simply not serious to fantasise about escaping from science and technology. Those who do fantasise in this way are only able to play with such ideas or hold them in their heads because scientific progress, from the first printing presses of the Renaissance onwards, has made popular education possible and set people sufficiently free from brute labour to have leisure to think.

Bronowski acknowledges that scientists have often enjoyed the power that has gone with being a favoured elite in society, and with dealing in knowledge that seems incomprehensible to those outside the elite, so that the rich and the powerful feel the need to flatter them, pay them well and above all seek their advice. Some scientists have been far from innocent and far from blameless in the situation in which a sharp rift has opened between science and the humanities on the one hand and between science and ordinary citizens on the other. Despite the valiant efforts of Bronowski and some other scientists in the last four decades the rift is still with us. Finally, he points out that the basis of science is 'the acceptance of what works and the rejection of what does not'. Nearly sixty years after Bronowski wrote his book we are clearly still failing to apply that simple test of what works and what does not ('That needs more courage than we might think'). We fail to apply it, for instance, to the world economy or to the laws we allow governments to impose on us or to the foreign policies they pursue, allegedly on our behalf.

### Science and Human Values (1956)

The style of this book is more playful, more sad, even bitter, and certainly more personal than *The Common Sense of Science*. This may be due to the fact that the three chapters that

make up *Science and Human Values* were originally given as
lectures at the Massachusetts Institute of Technology in
February and March 1953 when Bronowski was a visiting
professor there. In the first chapter Bronowski expands on
the theme of science as a creative act of the imagination. For
myself, I remember buying, at the age of fourteen or fifteen,
before I ever watched *The Ascent of Man*, a book by A.E.
Trueman called *Geology and Scenery in England and Wales* in
which the author insisted that the geologist must have an
eye and imagination equal to that of the artist and the poet.
At the time, of course, I found that statement difficult to
swallow; although I was certainly *interested* in geology, I
couldn't quite believe that it was comparable to
poetry — which, at the time, I was trying hard to write. Now,
after a lifetime of being influenced by Bronowski's thinking,
I don't find the statement at all difficult to accept. Scientific
laws and concepts begin with a courageous guess, and the
guess is directed towards finding likeness behind appearances that have suggested that there is no likeness at all.
They certainly do not begin with piling up mounds of facts
and observations. In 1543 someone brought Copernicus,
who was probably dying, the first printed copy of the book
he had written more than a decade earlier in which he stated
the thesis that the Earth moves around the sun. 'When did
Copernicus go out and record this fact with his camera?'
Bronowski asks. 'What [...] prompted his outrageous
guess? [And how] is this guess to be called a neutral record
of fact?' Kepler used metaphors and other analogies such as
relating the speeds of the planets to musical intervals in
searching for his laws of planetary motion, and in the twentieth century Niels Bohr and Ernest Rutherford made an
imaginative leap and found a model for the structure of the
atom in the orbit of the planets round the sun. And Newton,
sitting in his mother's garden and watching apples fall from
the tree to the ground, imagined the same force of gravity
that makes the apple fall stretching out into space and keep-
ing the Moon and the planets in their orbits. The falling
apple and the Moon seem astonishingly *unlike* each other,
but Newton found a new likeness, just as a poet does. A

good or great piece of poetry is striking because it makes new connections between the elements of reality. In *Romeo and Juliet* we find the line 'Death that hath sucked the honey of thy breath' spoken when Romeo finds Juliet and thinks that she is dead. Shakespeare rearranges the elements we expect to find in the world — not only has Death stung Juliet like a bee (a conventional enough image), it has come to her as if she were a flower, but it has sucked the honey of her breath *out of her*, whereas bees go to flowers in the everyday world to take the nectar out of which they *make* honey.

The scientist must, of course, work within a narrower frame of reference, within narrower boundaries than the poet and the artist, because scientific concepts must be tested against experienced, observable fact. Bronowski traces three stages in the process by which human beings build up their knowledge of the world — direct sense experience, a psychological mapping of the physical world, and the formation of concepts. Once again, in summarising his approach, I will offer some examples of my own to illustrate that approach. Young children will explore the physical world around them because they are stimulated to do so by direct sense experience, by seeing a picture that delights or frightens them, or by seeing their own reflections in a mirror. That exploration will lead to finding that on the other side of the picture is a blank piece of cardboard, and on the other side of the mirror is a drab wooden board, and usually the picture or the reflection cannot be seen at the same moment as the back of the picture or mirror. Next comes the realisation that the picture and its back are one object and the mirror and its back are one object, even though front and back cannot be seen at the same time, and whether we are children or adults, we make a psychological map of the object into which we fit the seen and the unseen side. Many animals can do this, recognising an object from whatever side they see it. However, from a very young age, human beings do something that other animals do not seem to be able to do. They form a *concept* of the object and hold it in their minds when it is not there to be seen or felt, being able to think about the object — or the person — when it, or he or she, has been absent for a long time. Not only can I recognise my wife when she returns after being away for a week, but I can also watch a film or read a book while she is away and make statements to myself such as 'My wife would be interested in this.' or 'My wife would find this funny.' or 'My wife would disapprove of this.' I fit what I see in the present into the overall concept I have of the person my wife is, even though she is not there to be seen. If my statements turn out to be wrong, then I conclude that I don't know her as well as I thought I did, and so I modify my concept of her accordingly. It is because we form concepts in this way that we can tell ourselves that this poem is in the style of Dylan Thomas, this singer is very like Madonna and this novel has the same atmosphere as *Wuthering Heights*, even when we haven't read any Dylan Thomas, or listened to Madonna's music or opened *Wuthering Heights* for months or even for years.

*   *   *

Bronowski suggests that the concepts of science, like other concepts, are checked against the facts we observe and experience and then corrected or modified. He returns to the logical positivists, who wanted to get away from concepts altogether and say that knowledge is built up of tiny units of facts that can be proved beyond any uncertainty, piece by piece, all logically following in sequence. He also glances at the operationalists who, following Ernst Mach in Austria and Percy Bridgman in America, assert that science is a series of observations or operations and should proceed by finding ways of measuring more of the universe more exactly. Bronowski goes out of his way to be fair to these two schools of thought by admitting that they have reason to be wary of concepts because the use of concepts has 'a bad record' that still corrupts and confuses talking in terms of concepts. It does indeed have a bad record — depending upon what period of history you look at! Concepts in the Middle Ages and since have too often been taken as self-evident or derived from some authority not to be challenged or arrived at by faith. St Thomas Aquinas held about two hundred and fifty discussion classes on the subject of truth between the years 1256 and 1259. The questions discussed included 'Is God's knowledge the cause of things?' and 'Is the Book of Life the same as predestination?' and 'Do angels know the future?' The concepts that are the starting point of such discussions are fixed, unchallenged and absolute, and they are never checked against experienced fact or against new facts and experiences, so that such discussions have nothing to do with the pursuit of truth or of a truthful approximate model of the world as we have understood it since the Scientific Revolution. Even in the seventeenth century the philosopher Baruch Spinoza (1632–77) wrote his book on *Ethics* 'proved in geometrical order', but we cannot have ethical or scientific concepts that are 'proved' for all time and fixed in stone in advance, summing up the universe, and never subject to being checked, corrected and modified, or at least, they will be of little use to us.

This correcting of concepts, this checking them against the facts that we see and experience is 'the habit of truth' as Bronowski calls it, and it has been with us since the Scientific Revolution. It is really the same as applying the simple test of what works and what does not work to the world around us. It is silly to pretend that we have applied this test to the political arrangements and laws that affect our lives or to foreign policies as often as we should or as rigorously as we should. However, that does not mean that Western societies have never applied this test to these affairs. Bronowski gives the example of Warren Hastings, who was impeached and tried in 1786 for the corruption of his rule in India. I would like to offer another example that is more recent. On April 15 1919 at Amritsar in India a British officer called General Dyer ordered his troops to open fire on an unarmed crowd of Indian demonstrators, killing 379 of them and leaving 1,200 of them wounded, including children. The commission of inquiry set up by the British severely censured Dyer and forced him to resign. Dyer had acted on fixed concepts of how Indians should be treated, so to speak, upon medieval concepts. Even in terms of British imperialism, these concepts had been long left behind, they 'would not work' even as methods to continue British rule in India, and they were condemned as such because the sensibility that had grown since the Scientific Revolution found them incompatible with sanity and morality. It is worth pointing out that there is a certain popular revisionism today regarding the slave trade. We are told that there was already slavery among Africans and that many slaves were sold to Europeans by other Africans. However, we have no need to judge the slave trade against these facts, instead we need to judge it by the sensibility we live by, as William Wilberforce did, we need to measure it against the sensibility and the concepts of the world that have grown up since the seventeenth century, and if we judge it by this sensibility we find it a crime and an abomination. It is worth recalling that the great physicist Heisenberg had to appeal to Himmler for protection from the SS, and when Himmler eventually decided to protect him, he felt Heisenberg to be a possible candidate for an Academy that Himmler was setting up—an Academy devoted to the conviction that the stars are made of ice. This, and also Auschwitz, are the consequences of deserting the sensibility and 'the habit of truth' that science has created.

Bronowski refers to the example of William Wilberforce (1759–1833) several times in *The Common Sense of Science* and *Science and Human Values*. However, I would like to pause at this point and quote Wilberforce more fully, as an example of the sensibility created by science expressing itself through one individual and entering the political life of society. Here is an abridged section of a speech given by Wilberforce to the House of Commons on May 12 1789:

> When I consider the magnitude of the subject I am to bring before the House—a subject in which the interests, not of this country, nor of Europe alone, but of the whole world, and of posterity, are involved: and when I think, at the same time, on the weakness of the advocate who has undertaken this great cause—when these reflections press upon my mind, it is impossible for me not to feel both terrified and concerned at my own inadequacy to such a task. But when I reflect, however, on the encouragement which I have had, through the whole course of a long and laborious

examination of this question, and how much candour I
have experienced, and how conviction has increased
within my own mind [...] I march forward with a firmer
step in the full assurance that my cause will bear me out,
and that I shall be able to justify on the clearest principles,
every resolution in my hand, the avowed end of which is
the total abolition of the slave trade. I wish [...] to guard
both myself and the House from entering into the subject
with any sort of passion. It is not their passions I shall
appeal to — I ask only for their cool and impartial reason
[...] I mean not to accuse anyone, but to take the shame
upon myself, in common, indeed, with the whole parliament of Great Britain, for having suffered this horrid trade
to be carried on under their authority.

This, I would suggest, is the voice of the civilisation that science has created in the last four centuries, a civilisation that
we are so accustomed to that we often ignore its values, perhaps forgetting that there is a desperate need to reassert
those values frequently.

In the third and final chapter of *Science and Human Values*
Bronowski asks again what values we live by, and indeed if
there *are* values that we can live by, and if there are, can science provide them? According to logical positivism, much
influenced by Bertrand Russell and the more recent analytical philosophy associated with Ludwig Wittgenstein
(1889–1951), one of the most admired philosophers of the
last few decades, all knowledge — as we have seen earlier — is built up from smaller, and certain, statements of
fact. Therefore, statements that contain the word *is* can be
verified, but moral or ethical statements, containing the
words *ought* or *should* can never be verified. Wittgenstein
later moved to the analytical approach, by which he considered the meaning of statements according to how they are
used socially, according to their significance to the people
who use them, and saw them in the light of the intentions of
individuals and the context of their statements. This
approach did not dismiss statements containing *ought* and
*should* as meaningless, but it very much tied their meaning
to the social situation, so that although they could not be
verified as logical steps of fact they could be defined by how
society is seen to use them and need them. This approach of

Wittgenstein was later applied, entertainingly but with dubious success, to the philosophy of religion by D.Z. Phillips of Swansea University. There is, however, a fallacy underlying logical positivism and analytical philosophy. How would Russell *alone* have been able to verify even a modest assertion such as, for example, that The Crab nebula is the dust of a supernova that exploded in 1054, and it glows because of the radioactive carbon created in the explosion? He would have to read and *believe* the historical research carried out by others, as well as accepting the findings of 'a sequence of instrument makers and astronomers and nuclear physicists, specialists in this and that' as Bronowski describes them. How would Wittgenstein *alone*, in the solitary contemplations expressed in his later writing — given that the material he drew on was social, literary and cultural — have been able to verify that phrases like 'the room was filled with the glory of God' or 'there was the smell of crookedness and deceit in the place' were intended in the way he believed they were intended or that they had the significance that he assumed they had? In order to *verify* the findings of his analysis Wittgenstein would have had to spend his whole lifetime in what anthropologists call fieldwork, or perhaps several lifetimes, given the breadth and range of his analysis. The logical positivist and the analytical philosopher must, in fact, rely on the words of others, as we all must, however much we test their words against common sense and ask if their words fit into a coherent whole with what we have read elsewhere.

* * *

As all our knowledge, from astrophysics to history, and even language itself has been built up communally, it follows that: 'there is a principle which binds society together, because without it the individual would be helpless to tell the true from the false. This principle is truthfulness.' So states Bronowski, adding that positivism and analytical philosophy, far from getting away from ethical and moral values as their followers want to do, are actually based on a moral obligation that Bronowski puts in italics: *'We OUGHT to act in such a way that what IS true can be verified to be so.'*

Bronowski then goes on to consider the society of scientists, stretching back as a community and a society into the early Renaissance,

> men and women who practise the sciences make a company of scholars which has been more lasting than any modern state, yet which has changed and evolved as no Church has.

He makes it clear that he is not claiming any special *personal goodness* in scientists as individuals, and indeed they are as varied as any social group, but as a society they have to live by certain values because of what they do. Other professions such as lawyers and doctors have rules and codes of conduct, but they do not spring directly from the work carried out by these professions. Science creates concepts and explores their consequences in the light of experience and facts, and so it must have 'the habit of truth' because it is the pursuit of truth, 'not as a dogma but as a process'. The values of science perform the task that is carried out by the idea of justice in human society — they negotiate a balance between the needs of the solitary individual and the individual as a member of society, something that Bronowski was to return to in *The Ascent of Man*. Scientists must believe in and uphold independence in the individual scientist, because independence is the mark of originality without which science could not continue, and they must uphold tolerance in the society of scientists collectively, because science cannot exist without tolerance for dissenting views or without safeguarding free enquiry, free thought, free speech. Tolerance must be based on respect, however, not upon indifference, and it is from the tension between independence and tolerance, these two primary values, that justice, due honour for the accomplishments of others, and respect between individuals derive. The society of scientists is based on what Bronowski calls 'the sense of human dignity'. He adds that the society of scientists has 'outlasted the empires of Louis XIV and the Kaiser' and goes on to the following moving passage:

In [science] who now holds the beliefs that seemed firm sixty years ago? Yet the society of scientists has survived these changes without a revolution, and honours the men whose beliefs it no longer shares. No one has been shot or exiled or convicted of perjury; no one has recanted abjectly at a trial before his colleagues.

Clearly, Bronowski regards the values of science and the way in which scientists have been able to make their own society work as highly as any discoveries made about the world or the practical, liberating benefits that have been brought to the human race. He does, however, in his enthusiasm for these values take a quotation from William Clifford (1845–79) that raises interesting moral questions.

If I steal money from any person, there may be no harm done [...] But I cannot help doing this great wrong to Man, that I make myself dishonest. What hurts society is not that it should lose its property, but that it should become a den of thieves; for then it must cease to be society. This is why we ought not to do evil that good may come; for at any rate this great evil has come, that we have done evil and are made wicked thereby.

Bronowski adds: 'This is the scientist's moral: that there is no distinction between ends and means.' But is this true, and is it completely compatible with Bronowski's own life and work as a scientist? During the Second World War he worked on pioneering methods of operational research that used mathematics to increase the effectiveness of bombing raids and their economic impact. Therefore, his work was directly involved in the strategic bombing of Germany. The defeat of Hitler was necessary to the continuation of civilisation and necessary to prevent the expansion of the Holocaust, claiming, as it would have done, still more millions of innocent lives, and so the strategic bombing of Germany can be justified on these grounds. The dropping of the atomic bombs on Japan, on the other hand, was not inevitable or necessary. Nevertheless, the strategic bombing of Germany reached such proportions that Churchill exclaimed, when watching a film of the raids: 'Are we beasts? Are we taking this too far?' This incident is described by Paul Addison in his biography of Churchill, drawing on earlier sources. There was surely nothing 'good' about the deaths of so many German civilians, and it was indeed a case of 'doing evil that good may come'. Bronowski himself reminds us in *The Common Sense of Science*: 'We have preached [high moral precepts] too long to men who are forced to live how they can.' A nation, or an alliance of nations, is also forced to live how it can when fighting for its survival and the survival of civilisation, against Hitler, one of 'the two great catastrophes of the twentieth century' (as Bronowski called him). It seems that on this occasion Bronowski recoils from the bluntness of George Orwell:

> You can let the Nazis rule the world; that is evil; or you can overthrow them by war, which is also evil. There is no other choice before you, and whichever you choose you will not come out with clean hands.

Finally, of course, it is for the individual reader to grapple with this question.

### *The Identity of Man* (1965)

The first chapter of this book deals with precisely the question of human identity and with the impact of a certain awareness that science has brought to us, which still haunts us today. By the seventeenth century it had become clear that the heavens above us were not made of some special, unearthly material — instead, the same matter made up the Earth, the planets, the stars and the bodies of human beings and other animals. That last phrase *human beings and other animals*, the realisation that human beings and other animals have all evolved from a common stock of ancestors became the next phase in the troubling awareness that science created. Charles Darwin did not invent the theory of evolution, his grandfather Erasmus Darwin was quite familiar with it, and, in one shape or form or another the concept had been around for centuries. Charles Darwin found the mechanism that drove evolution on, which he called natural selection. The genetic material in living things is frequently throwing up variations, and one variation or several variations will turn out to be better adapted to the environment than the others, and as well as this, the environment changes greatly over millions of years and is different in different parts of the planet, so that in spreading over the Earth living things spread into new environments. The better adapted variations survive because they gain more of the food supply, live longer and have more offspring; and they continue to change and adapt, so that over huge periods of time animals and plants are found that bear so little resemblance to their remote ancestors that the common origin of all life is not obvious to the eye. More complex living things also tend to survive better than less complex ones, so that there is a constant movement in evolution from simple to complex organisms.

Once Darwin had established the driving mechanism of evolution it was accepted by scientists and has generally been accepted by society. Certain religious groups find it incompatible with their beliefs, but I shall happily pass over this dispute in silence. The uneasiness caused by the two aspects of this awareness — the fact that the same matter makes up the whole universe and ourselves and that we are animals descended from the same common ancestors as all other animals — cannot be passed over in silence. Gradually, a third realisation has spread. The same atoms make up a rock, a cat, a dog or a human being, and the only crucial difference is that they are arranged in a different architecture. You and I are an assembly of atoms obeying natural laws, just as a star is, and further, our brains and bodies and the brains and bodies of other animals, as well as the genetic material we pass on from parent to child, are all interlocking constellations of atoms. There is something in all this that displeases us and does not satisfy us. The influence of Christianity, the influence of religions and philosophies far older than Christianity, and the sensibility that has grown up since the Scientific Revolution have all instilled in us the wish to be persons, free agents, and each of us wants to be a *self* and to be *unique*.

Bronowski calls this uneasiness

> the explosive charge which in this century has split open
> the self-assurance of western man [...] that troubles yet
> silences us [...] gnaws at us still [...] nags at our self-esteem
> [we] have uneasily pushed this thought out of [our] heads.

He goes on to state serenely that 'what I shall construct by
way of an answer is a philosophy for modern man.' (No
wonder that he had quarrelled with Laura Riding and that
Robert Graves had secretly loathed him way back in 1934!)
Bronowski begins by confronting 'the crisis of confidence
which springs from [our] wish to be a mind and a person, in
the face of the nagging fear that we are mechanisms.' He
asks what it is to be unique and to be a self. We are all biolog-
ically unique, which is why human organ transplants are
difficult and sometimes fail — the body rejects the transplant
as part of its defence against invading proteins, and the bodies of almost all other vertebrate animals (those having a
backbone) do the same. The exceptions are identical twins
who can accept grafts from each other, and yet identical
twins also want to be, and manifestly are, separate selves.
However, it is not necessary to be born unique in order to be
unique. Machines become unique. After a year or two of
use, as every driver knows, two cars of the same model will
develop their own peculiarities, oddities, and their own dis-
tinctive sounds, and in detective stories and in real life people were caught because their typewriters, originally
identical to thousands of others, had worn in a certain way,
forming letters in a recognisably different way from other
typewriters. I can remember that when people used foun-
tain pens much more they were often reluctant to lend them
to someone else — the nib had worn in a way that suited the
slant of the owner's handwriting, and he or she did not want
that reshaped by another hand. And yet biological uniqueness and the uniqueness of machines do not satisfy our wish
to be unique selves. Further, as I pointed out at the beginning of this chapter, Bronowski also rejects the
existentialists' authentic, freely choosing individual as too
subjective and too self-defeatingly cut off from nature and
from history.

If we want to escape from the fear that we are mechanical, then the uncertainty built into the world is not much comfort here either—the processes of nature can be called mechanical, although they cannot be predicted with certainty. The principle of uncertainty would only seem to make us less predictable, so that our future actions are only probable and not certain, but this does not make us into selves. When the quantum physicist tells me that I will not act in exactly the same way tomorrow as I have today, because it is overwhelmingly improbable that my environment can repeat itself exactly, or when I am told that a particular environment (even if it *could* repeat itself exactly) may touch off any one of a whole range of actions, I am still not reassured that this makes me a self.

Bronowski reaches the core of his argument when he points out the simple and elegant truth that we shall be different tomorrow from today because of the experiences that will have been added to the total sum of our experiences. I shall be an expanded self tomorrow, and more so next week and next year, just as I am a larger self than I was a week ago or a year ago. This is Bronowski's radical conclusion: we all do indeed have a self, a unique self, not as a fixed and static thing, but as a *process* of turning our experiences into knowledge and into the self. As human beings we are also capable of forming concepts, of working with images, so that we have a life of the imagination, which means we have inner experiences. 'In recall, in fantasy, in speculation, and in foresight [we have] experiences which do not happen—that is, which are not outward events.' My experience, and yours, and that of every person, whether inward or outward is unique, and so is the process by which we turn experience into knowledge.

In order to make this radical conclusion sharper and give it greater depth Bronowski returns to the definition of a machine, which is not as self-evident as it is often thought to be. At first sight the definition is very obvious—press the button or pull the lever and the machine performs some action or other. This description only fits very simple machines, but in the world of modern computers, and even the world of the earliest computers or predicting machines, the description will not do. For sophisticated machines, Bronowski traces three steps that form a procedure, and the machine *is* the procedure, all three steps of it. First, there is the instruction or input, 'the modern form of the button that starts the machine', which must be precise and mechanical, something that can be recorded as 'marks on a tape' (Bronowski's words here already sound old-fashioned and antiquated today, but his grasp of essential principles is still relevant). Next comes the physical machinery, the circuits that carry out the instruction or process the input. Thirdly, there is the result or output, 'which is equally decisive and definite', something that, we would say today, can be stored on a computer's hard drive. Computers need to regulate themselves, and to correct and instruct themselves, so that the output must be as 'exact and unambiguous' as the input is, 'as well defined and single-minded as its input'.

If the self is a process by which experience is turned into knowledge, can the self be called a kind of machine? Here Bronowski draws a distinction that is vital to his book and to his entire philosophy. There are two ways in which human beings turn experience into knowledge. One way is through science, which Bronowski calls one mode of knowledge, and the present level of scientific knowledge could be stored on a computer and could be tested by experiment. There is, however, as he tells us, another mode of knowledge that is knowledge of the self, and this cannot be stored or recorded by any kind of machine that we can imagine. I have slightly altered the appealing illustration of the two kinds of knowledge that Bronowski gives at the end of the first chapter of *The Identity of Man* in order to make it more concise. I can decide that I won't raise my glass tomorrow in the same way as I did today because I spilled wine on my wife's dress. That was merely a physical error, and a knowledge of Newton's laws — laws that can be formally recorded and stored by a machine — can prevent the error, so that this decision belongs to the scientific mode of knowledge. But I can also decide that I won't raise my glass in that way again because last time it embarrassed my wife. The second decision belongs to knowledge of the self because it is based on recognising my wife's embarrassment and imagining how it would feel if I felt it. No machine is capable of this recognition or this act of imagination, and no machine could record or store them, yet knowledge of the self is 'real and powerful in human affairs' as Bronowski reminds us.

Bronowski would have been excited, had he lived, by the wonderful discussion of the biological origin of morality and altruistic behaviour by Richard Leakey, who had spent many years studying early human evolution around Lake Turkana in Kenya, in his *Origins Reconsidered: In Search of What Makes Us Human* (1992). Leakey points out that human beings at an early stage of evolution *competed within their own groups* for a greater share of food, status and sexual favours and used forms of tactical deception to do so, just as chimpanzees, gorillas and baboons do. This capacity to play a kind of social chess game for advantage against members of the same species does not seem to be possessed by any other animal, and naturally it is played best by those individuals who can guess what a rival will do next, while those who can guess what a rival is *feeling* will guess more accurately. With the development of the hunter-gatherer way of life, human society became more complex and the benefits of winning the social chess game became greater, and those humans with the ability to imagine the feelings of others most clearly were favoured. As human society became more sophisticated, cooperation became ever more important and rules of conduct and a sense of justice were needed to balance the needs of the individual and the needs of the community. The ability to imagine the pain or happiness of others could never be removed once it had developed in human beings, and as the capacity to think in the abstract grew with it, we acquired altruism and a moral sense. Human beings possess compassion—in the original sense of *feeling with*—for sound biological reasons. Leakey's discussion enriches and extends Bronowski's philosophy, and both reassert that a human being is a self and not a machine.

Science is a living language for talking about nature, and every so often scientists invent new words, as with the word 'electron' coined by J.J. Thomson in 1897. Electrons are real in the sense that their behaviour can be described and observed, but an electron is not a *thing*, in any ordinary sense of the word thing. The concepts that science creates and the picture of nature that it builds up are real enough, although they are partial explanations, and it is amazing that the explanations work so well. As Bronowski was to say later: 'Science is a tribute to what we can know although we are fallible' (*The Ascent of Man*). Every real, living language, however, contains some ambiguity. We cannot precisely define what an electron is, let alone measure its speed and position simultaneously, and we cannot exactly define the meaning of any word, but this does not prevent the words of a poem fitting together into a meaningful whole. Science also has its ambiguity, although scientific laws are written out in a way that keeps ambiguity to a minimum — the present state of scientific knowledge has to be tested in action at any given moment, and so an explanation in science has to give instructions for that testing. Beyond the tests made at any given moment, of course, scientists are not obliged to regard the present state of knowledge as closed and fixed, and they cannot do so if they are to remain scientists. Scientific thinking is, therefore, just as much an imaginative act as poetry, but whereas poetry relishes and exploits ambiguity, because it does not set out to give instructions, scientific explanations get rid of as much ambiguity as possible.

When a concept such as phlogiston (once believed to be part of anything combustible, to be released in combustion) no longer fits in with the connected framework of laws that make up the scientific picture of the world, it is thrown away. When an experiment such as measuring the position of the planet Mercury proves that Relativity is a better picture of the universe than classical Newtonian physics, then one picture replaces the other. No scientist goes on believing that phlogiston both does and does not exist, and no scientist goes on believing that Relativity and Newtonian physics are equally good pictures of the world. Scientific knowledge is exclusive and unambiguous. However, literature, which is one of the main sources of knowledge of the self, is not like this at all. Here I will mainly give my own examples from literature, rather than Bronowski's, because I think that mine are more accessible and closer to the tastes of our own time. The poem *And Death Shall Have No Dominion* by Dylan Thomas is not a religious sermon on immortality and it is not a scientific prediction about processes that may happen after a person's heartbeat and breathing have stopped, and yet it certainly gives us knowledge because it is in itself an emotional experience. Similarly, another poem by Dylan Thomas, *Do Not Go Gentle Into That Good Night* is not a List of Rules of Etiquette or a Code of Conduct for those individuals whose heartbeat and breathing are about to cease. And when Macbeth comes to his final, bleak, nihilistic conclusion:

> Tomorrow, and tomorrow, and tomorrow,
> Creeps in this petty pace from day to day,
> To the last syllable of recorded time:
> And all our yesterdays have lighted fools
> The way to dusty death. Out, out, brief candle,
> Life's but a walking shadow, a poor player,
> That struts and frets his hour upon the stage,
> And then is heard no more. It is a tale
> Told by an idiot, full of sound and fury
> Signifying nothing.

Shakespeare is not asking us to 'agree' with him or to approve of his actions, but instead to see ourselves in Macbeth and see Macbeth in ourselves. Macbeth's words are no more 'true' or 'false' than Miranda's exclamation in *The Tempest* (in the story she is speaking sincerely and without irony:) 'O brave new world,/That has such people in it.' Even literature (rather than entertainment or political speeches disguised as literature) that has a definite, translatable message does not invite approval or agreement. George Orwell's novel *Nineteen Eighty-Four* was certainly written to influence society and politics in one direction rather than in others, and yet its central character Winston Smith, who rebels against the totalitarian state of Big Brother, is not 'right' or 'wrong' or 'strong' or 'weak', and the chief interrogator and torturer O'Brien is not a 'monster' in the cheap thriller or tabloid newspaper sense of the word, and if the characters were portrayed like this, then the book would have been forgotten decades ago. The novel calls us into its imaginative world so that we can see our own world more clearly.

Although Bronowski does not deal with religious literature in *The Identity of Man*, I would like to give some space to considering the New Testament at this point. The Gospels, however accurately or inaccurately they record the life and words of Jesus, are great literature because they possess an amazing dramatic tension and economy of style. It is astonishing to reflect that some of the most famous statements attributed to Jesus are *not* prescriptions or rules for conduct at all, but rather passionate appeals to those who heard them to look into themselves and find answers. When we read of the woman taken in adultery, 'in the very act', being brought to Jesus we sense the masculine cruelty and excitement of her accusers behind the terse verses of the story — an excitement that was of course the outward expression of *their own* lust for her. Jesus does not debate with them or even tell them that they are wrong, only saying: 'He that is without sin among you, let him first cast a stone at her.' It is enough to make the excited men slink away one by one, being 'convicted by *their own* conscience' (John 8. 7–9). When asked whether Jews should pay taxes to Rome Jesus said: 'Render to Caesar the things that are Caesar's, and to God the things that are God's' (Mark 12.14–17). He did not define what was God's and what was Caesar's, which is to say that he did not spell out the extent to which we should cooperate with the power of governments, leaving that to our own consciences — and it is certainly as urgent a question today as it ever was.

When George Eliot makes her heroine Dorothea Brooke marry the hideous Mr Casaubon in *Middlemarch* she is not writing a health warning to young women, but asking us to sympathise with the urge that most of us have at some time — to be heroic and self-sacrificing in a society that offers very little scope for greatness. Yes, Doris Lessing's Anna Wulf in *The Golden Notebook* is frequently irritating as she grapples with problems of creativity, political loyalty and sexuality, and so are the people around us, just as we often irritate them. Bronowski writes:

> By contrast, literature does not try to provoke in us the response of action, and therefore does not need to resolve its ambiguities. We feel ourselves within all the actors of the drama, and we are not asked to judge their behaviour by its effectiveness. We are not asked to judge their behaviour at all [...] But it is by no means evident that we know how to act better in any specific encounter. [...] There are no morals in a poem; there are no morals in any work of art. [...] And by identifying ourselves with the experience of others, we enlarge our knowledge of ourselves as human beings: we gain self-knowledge.

It is precisely this kind of knowledge that Bronowski insists, quite rightly I believe, is something that cannot be stored or recorded on any kind of machine that we can imagine.

Human identity is for Bronowski what we *do*, which is to build up these two kinds of knowledge, scientific knowledge and self-knowledge, and this is the 'total philosophy' that he offers. The values of tolerance and respect for others necessary in science are also among the intimate values that we need in personal and social life, and they form a bridge between the two sets of values. Respect also creates self-respect because we see ourselves in others to some extent. It must be said that thirty-five years after Bronowski's death we have hardly begun to pull scientific knowledge and self-knowledge together into a coherent set of values. Worse still, we have on one side the confident assertions of political and religious leaders that *their* groups are both right and superior, and on the other side our personal loyalties to our friends and families, and perhaps to our immediate communities. There is very little of the pride and confidence that shine through all Bronowski's work—the pride in being human and confidence in ourselves as a species and in our future. That pride and confidence were severely undermined at the place at which I began this book, Auschwitz, and at Hiroshima and Nagasaki, and they continue to be undermined by almost every dose of the daily news about what is going on in the world. We need to regain the awareness that Auschwitz, Hiroshima and Nagasaki, as well as the awful abuses of the twenty-first century were, and are, made possible not by science but by the desertion of the 'habit of truth' on which science has been built.

### *The Origins of Knowledge and Imagination* (1978)

I shall not devote as much space to the other works by Bronowski considered here. In his later books he expanded upon and refined his philosophy, but he did not significantly add to it or change it. In *The Ascent of Man*, of course, he dramatised his ideas and made them more accessible than ever before, and yet I shall not give it the greatest amount of space because most of my present book has been, in one way or another, a commentary on *The Ascent of Man*. Despite its forbidding title, *The Origins of Knowledge and Imagination* is one of his most entertaining and fast-paced works. The six chapters were originally given as Mrs Hepsa Ely Silliman lectures at Yale in 1967, and Bronowski intended them to form one of a pair of books, a project that was disrupted by the making of *The Ascent of Man*, so that he never revised the lectures as a book, leaving the published text as the transcript of the lectures, even including slips of the tongue that were rapidly turned into jokes. In the lectures he set himself the task of seeing through the enterprise proposed by the philosopher Immanuel Kant (1724–1804) in the 1760s, 'to construct a natural philosophy which was based on the physical ability of human beings to receive and translate their experience of the outside world'. This was an admirable project for a natural philosopher, as Bronowski always called himself, especially when we consider how many philosophers have approached the world abstractly, inside their own heads, instead of going to the actual workings of human biology.

The book begins with the sense of sight, emphasising how important it is to human beings and other primates such as the apes, and yet the apes cannot discriminate fine detail as we can. Further, words connected with sight—'vi-

sion', 'visionary', 'image', 'imagery', 'imagination' permeate all our thinking about art and our experiences, both
inner and outer. We would expect, therefore, that the
human eye has developed as a sort of superior optical
instrument. However, this is not the case. The rods and
cones in the eye and the nerves that lead back to the brain
are really rather coarse, and yet amazingly *they* sort out and
group light and dark and movement into meaningful
shapes and patterns *before* sending messages to the brain.
The eye is not a camera sending passive images that the
brain sorts out, but instead it is pre-wired to look for and to
impose a sort of order. We never only see red — we see red
things, patches of red and red shapes. Even this is too crude
a description of sight because our picture of the world is
formed by a kind of conversation or dialogue between the
eye sending selected patterns and the brain that has formed
certain categories. Bronowski had insisted in *The Identity of
Man* that our picture of the world 'is not the look of the
world but our way of looking at it, not how the world strikes
us but how we construct it'.

In the second chapter of *The Origins* Bronowski considers
the other ability that, like the sense of sight, is vastly more
highly developed in human beings than in our fellow animals, the gift of language. Other animals communicate with
each other, and some of them do so in a quite complex and
sophisticated way, so that the number of varied statements
they are able to make is considerable. Non-human animals,
however, speak in *sentences*, and their statements convey
practical information only, such as warnings of danger or
the announcement that a good food supply has been found.
Animals such as dogs may be an exception, as I would add
from my own experience, because through long association
with humans they may imitate human words — and the context of the words to some extent — in a form of communication that is non-canine and beyond the merely practical. We
might look at the following sentences. 'Science and poetry
were the ideal lifetime pursuits for Jacob.' 'Jacob found that
science and poetry were ideal lifetime pursuits.' The first
striking thing is that although the sentences are close in

meaning, they do not have the *same meaning*, and secondly, if we have no other information about Jacob, the sentences suggest other statements and questions. Did Jacob have the insight to realise that they were ideal lifetime pursuits? Although he found that science and poetry were ideal for him, did something prevent his life being devoted to them? Other animals could only manage these sentences. 'Hey, Jacob! I've found some science and poetry over here, come and get some!' 'Careful, Jacob, that hungry lion is between you and the science and poetry!' I am, of course, pushing the example to the point of caricature and impossibility – as Bronowski sometimes liked to do – because no other animal is able to use abstract concepts such as 'science' or 'poetry', or to speak of the past. It is just as fundamental to point out that animal sentences are fixed, whereas we can separate the words 'found' and 'lion' and 'between' and understand them perfectly well in isolation. Humans can distinguish words that stand for objects and actions and use and understand them even when they do not refer to any actual situation, and we can also carry on internal conversations with ourselves. Bronowski sees human language as evolving in a continuous process from animal communication, and he quotes the Gospel of Saint John, 'In the beginning was the Word…' (1. 1), and yet wonderful as this is as a concept, it is not a description of what happened in human evolution. In the beginning was the sentence – at least in evolutionary terms. The Gospel of John goes on to state the miracle in religious terms, 'And the Word was made flesh…' (1. 14) In scientific terms the marvel is that natural selection, as well as human culture and society, the driving mechanisms of evolution caused the words to fall out of the sentence.

Newton's statement that the gravitational pull between two massive bodies falls off at a regular rate over the distance between them, that is to say that the Moon is like a ball being thrown around the Earth 250,000 miles above us, is a daring piece of visualisation and imagination, and yet he turned his metaphor into an algorithm, which is a formula that can be calculated. Of course, every piece of imagination like this, and the experiments that back it up, disregard the fact that everything in the universe is totally connected and that everything influences everything else. Newton's picture and his calculations, like every scientific picture, draw a line around one piece of the universe and say that only certain things are relevant, but nevertheless, as with Newton, good approximate laws can be found in this way.

There is a rather more disturbing consequence of violating the total connectedness of the universe. In mathematics and in logic some propositions can never be proved to be true or false, and in mathematics particularly there are times when there are no shortcuts to finding an answer, no procedure, and no rule. There are some propositions that can only be tested by making one calculation after another endlessly, with no way of predicting if one day you will find an answer that is an exception. We can only ever examine a part or an aspect of nature at any one time, and so we cannot escape from our own finiteness, and we are locked into the shape that the very language we use imposes on us. In ancient Greek literature the problem was brought out by the paradox of Epimenides the Cretan who said: 'All Cretans are liars.' And was he telling the truth? Bertrand Russell, referred to earlier, ran into just this problem in his work on mathematics and logic and he states in his autobiography: 'It seemed unworthy of a grown man to spend his time on such trivialities, but what was I to do?' The problem is a real one because human beings have desperately wanted to discover the definite laws that would explain the universe step by step, logically and strictly, and they have believed that the laws are there to be discovered, entirely outside themselves.

We might ask how, as a species, we have been able to do science and mathematics and build as good a picture of the universe as the one we have. The reason that Bronowski suggests is that we are not bound by these paradoxes and uncertainties precisely because we are *not* abstract, fixed selves sitting inside our brains and receiving messages, sorting them out and sending orders to our muscles — this is the notion that goes back to the philosopher Descartes and before. If we functioned like this, then the brain would work like a digital computer. However, as Bronowski's friend Johnny von Neumann pointed out, the brain does not work like this—it does not have enough accuracy, and if it had that much accuracy it would not have enough memory. Instead, the sense organs such as the eye, the nerves, the muscles and the brain are one whole and they work as one whole. The brain seems to use some kind of statistical language unlike any statistical language that we know, that is, that we have consciously and outwardly invented. We may never *know* how the brain works in any exact sense, and yet, as with physics, we may build a better and better picture of the processes of the brain. Bronowski suggests the clue of likening the brain to a gas compressed to half its volume so that the pressure doubles because, statistically, the number of times that the speeding atoms in the gas will collide with the inside of the container will double. The collisions of the gas atoms may be something like the huge amount of connections and cross-references in the brain, so that input to the brain (we should probably say input to the eye, senses, nerves, brain and muscles together) is something like compressing a gas, bringing more and more of these connections into play. The brain does not rely, therefore, on super-fast computing but on the immense number of connections and cross-references it has inside it, and therefore it copes with—it seems to thrive on—uncertainty and ambiguity, although a highly interconnected uncertainty. Human language reflects the uncertainty and ambiguity that the brain deals in all the time; after all, we cannot define any word absolutely precisely and we cannot make any statement that is absolutely clear-cut and free from ambiguity. This seems to explain why we go on doing science and art, building pictures of the world and eventually accepting their incompleteness and then seeking better ones. The brain has evolved so that it is able to deal with errors, and to use errors, both in scientific knowledge and in the knowledge of the self.

Bronowski's final chapter is devoted to repeating, to a large extent, his discussion of the scientific ethic given in

*Science and Human Values*, and he acknowledges this, confronting once again the issue that while the findings of science are ethically neutral, the practice of science is not. Science is devoted to finding out what 'is', but in order to find this out, we 'ought' to act in such a way that the truth can be found. He also considers once again the values that have been absolutely necessary to the community of scientists since the seventeenth century, such as independence, tolerance, respect and dignity. He adds that we all live in a society penetrated through and through by the scientific outlook, by 'the habit of truth'. In one way or another almost everyone sees that in politics, national and international, there is not a 'credibility gap' but a 'hypocrisy gap'. This was written in 1967, and it is even more true today when politicians have come to be regarded, almost by definition, as liars, so that the rupture between governments and the rest of us is alarming, and perhaps beyond repair.

## The Ascent of Man (1973)

It is, of course, only fitting to consider the television series and the book together, forming the culmination of Bronowski's work and the richest and most intense expression of his ideas, although we can only see them as the culmination of his career in retrospect, because he happened to die the year after the series was first screened, at the age of sixty-six. We do not know what work he might have done if he had lived longer or how he might have reacted to developments in science or events in the world in general. When viewers first watched *The Ascent of Man*, the Watergate scandal that would destroy the presidency of Richard Nixon was convulsing American society and the Apollo programme of Moon landings was already over, and at the same time the Soviet Union was moving towards the peak of its success as a world power, ruled by an aging bureaucracy that was still intolerant of criticism or freedom of expression. The reforms of Soviet society under Gorbachev were far away and the eventual collapse of the Soviet bloc was barely imaginable, just as the rise of the neo-conservatives in America was unforeseen. In Britain and all across the industrialised world there were soon to be events that would send the world in a new direction—away from the expanding prosperity and optimism of the 1960s. Bronowski's resolute optimism was one of the defining voices of the seventies, the note of faith in human abilities that he sounded competed with other, and contradictory, messages. Those who watched the series (and still watch it) cannot help being struck by the originality and daring of a guide through history and evolution that moves from the ruins of the Inca empire to ancient Greece, from Moorish Spain to the eccentric scientists of the Industrial revolution, from the poetry of Blake to the concentration camp, from Palaeolithic cave paintings to the laboratory, from Galileo to *Hamlet*, and from Easter Island to Einstein envisaging what it would be like to travel on a beam of light at the speed of light while actually travelling on a Swiss tram. The scene constantly shifted, sometimes from one minute to the next within the programmes.

Bronowski strode through all these places, a short man with a kindly face and impeccable English with a faint Eastern European tinge, often making jokes and once moved to tears, and if he said very little that was new about his philosophy—explaining his term *stratified stability* was an exception—he said it more grippingly and reached more millions than he had reached before. The magnificent variety on the television screen and the gorgeous, lavish quality of the book made a lasting impression, and the bounding optimism about the future was tempered by the warning of Auschwitz in the past and a loss of nerve in the present. There was nothing fixed about Bronowski's vision of the future.

> Every so often some visionary invents a new Utopia: Plato, Sir Thomas More, H. G. Wells. [...] That is not the essence of the human personality [...] Biologically, a human being is changeable, sensitive, mutable, fitted to many environments, and not static. The real vision of the human being is the child wonder, the Virgin and Child, the Holy Family.

In describing an edition of the works of Hippocrates printed by Frobenius in the 1500s he says 'the happy passion of the printer sits on the page as powerful as the knowledge'. Bronowski used the words 'happy passion' more than once in his work. It is that quality, above all others, that is the key-note of *The Ascent of Man*.

### *The Visionary Eye* (1978)

This book was compiled by Rita Bronowski and Piero E. Ariotti and first published four years after Bronowski's death, and it demonstrates not only his passion for poetry but also his skill as a critic and commentator on poetry. It beautifully expands on some of his previous ideas, notably the abiding theme of his work—that imagination is just as much a part of science as it is of poetry. Scientists look at the particulars of nature and make a leap forward towards laws (that must be tested by experiment) but poetry is different in that the particulars of its imagery are what make it immedi-ately universal and able to speak to all of us. In poetry, so to speak, the particulars *are* the universal laws. I would add from my own experience that attempts at poetry that leave out concrete, sensuous images are flat statements or at best sermons. If we reduce *The Force That Through the Green Fuse Drives the Flower* by Dylan Thomas to a simple statement of its message, that is, when you are young, growing older is wonderful, but when you are old, growing older is tragic, then it strikes us as mildly clever and wise or perhaps mildly depressing. It is the language of the poem that makes us experience the statement for ourselves. It has always seemed to me that Gloucester's bitter remark in *King Lear*, when reduced to a statement, is depressing, but most of all dull: Life is cruel and we are tortured for fun. Shakespeare's actual lines produce a different effect. 'As flies to wanton boys, are we to the Gods,/They kill us for their sport.' It is the particular, concrete image that makes us experience once again the emotion that goes with a thought we have all entertained at times, however fleetingly. Further, a poem is a slightly different experience for all of us, and to appreciate it we must recreate the poem for ourselves, and recreate for ourselves the poet's excitement in writing it, so that your experience of the poem will be somewhat different from mine. Properly to understand a scientific discovery or a scientific law is also to recreate the excitement of the discovery for ourselves. Science is also full of particulars and concrete images, such as Newton's apples and his metaphor of the Moon being a ball thrown around and around the Earth 250,000 miles above us. Bronowski wonderfully answers a frequently asked question: Must not a scientific theory be true, and may not a work of art be quite untrue? A scientific theory must fit the facts that can be observed at the time it is formulated, and yet Einstein showed that Newton's theory never had been *true* in any obvious sense. As for works of art being quite untrue, I would like to expand on Bronowski's answer by pointing out the following. There are a great many novels and books of poems on the shelves of bookshops that are untrue, not because their contents are *invented* (which is usual), but because they don't have any truths about ourselves or about life to tell us. We read them, if we read them, to kill time and all we have at the end of them is the sense 'that time has been killed' as the critic F.R. Leavis put it. This, I suggest, is curiously passive. And Bronowski stresses in the essays in *The Visionary Eye* that his aesthetic approach is an active one, so that abstract questions such as 'What is beauty?' or 'How do we judge what is beautiful?' are misplaced. The question should be 'Why do human beings exert themselves to produce something that seems beautiful to themselves or others?' He returns to the gifts of language and imagination that have made human beings freer than any other animal. Both cultural and biological evolution have moved in the direction of greater and greater freedom and choice. Art has its roots in practical invention, and the creation of art is an exercise in freedom, just as inventions, from stone tools onwards, have been. When we *actively* recreate for ourselves the work of art we also take pleasure in the exercise of freedom.

### *Journey Round a Twentieth Century Skull*
### (The last broadcasts)

The broadcasts were a series of conversations recorded between George Steedman and Bronowski after the making of *The Ascent of Man*. They were later transmitted on BBC Radio 3 and Radio 4 and by the World Service, and published in the magazine *The Listener* between May 15 and July 3 1975. Steedman begins by suggesting that 'an archaeologist in some distant future might dig up our skulls and somehow be able to discern what had been the specific content of our twentieth century minds.' Bronowski brings out the point by contrasting the content of 'my father's skull — a nineteenth century skull' with that of his own. Three great discoveries overthrew the nineteenth century view of nature between 1897 and 1927 — firstly, it was found that the atom was not the smallest constituent of matter, secondly, it became apparent that energy also comes in lumps or packets called quanta and that the universe moves in unexpected quantum leaps, and thirdly, due to Einstein, it was understood that we cannot separate ourselves from the universe we observe, so that we are always part of the observation. Heisenberg's principle of uncertainty of 1927 further revolutionised human understanding of the universe.

Bronowski is at his most relaxed during these conversations, and his excitement about science, as well as his geniality and sense of fun light up the serious and sometimes difficult concepts he is explaining. One of these is that, with the discovery of the neutron, it became clear that atoms — and therefore all matter — evolve from simple types to very complex ones, just as life evolves from simple forms to complex ones. The fusion of hydrogen to make helium in the Sun is the fundamental example of this. Living things are special because the architecture of the atoms that make them up allows them to constantly replicate themselves when cells divide and when cells unite to become a future creature, although the atoms themselves are identical to the atoms that make up non-living matter. Strangely, more complex forms of life cope with the disturbances of nature better than simple ones, the multicellular animal copes

better than simple, single-cell life forms. Bronowski contin-
ues:

> Dots make a letter, letters make a word, words make a sen-
> tence, sentences make paragraphs, paragraphs make chap-
> ters, chapters make a book. [...] There is obviously
> something very deep about the laws of nature [...] complex
> things hold together by virtue of their organisation — even
> though their simple units are the ultimate building blocks
> to which they would otherwise fall.

At one point, speaking of politics, Bronowski makes a
scathing expression of aloof disdain.

> I do not care what is going on in 10 Downing Street, in the
> White House, in Jerusalem and Cairo, which seems so
> important to the newspapers.

Science and poetry, he maintains, will shape the future of
the human race far more than 'those silly political decisions'. We may well agree with him, in the long term, but he
may also have contradicted himself. The rise of Hitler, one
of 'the two great catastrophes of the twentieth century' also
began with 'silly political decisions'. Political power may be
an illusion, but as Auschwitz and Hiroshima prove, it can
be a very powerful illusion for long enough to do terrible
harm. He goes on to speak of his own work at the Salk Institute, of trying to bring scientific knowledge and the knowledge of the self that comes from literature and art together
into a new understanding of what human beings are.

> I do not run around and dissect rabbits or tell people how to
> make pigeons peck at targets, or rats run mazes [...]
> pigeons and rats are wonderful but not at all lovable [...] I
> do not believe in any of that [...] I am in love with the
> human race [...] Let's talk about a nice, good animal like a
> dog. Dogs are nice. They are really very nice. [...] Dogs are
> very smart. They have quite elaborate habits [...]

Bronowski embarks on a humorous discussion of whether
dogs have, in fact, adapted human beings to their needs,
rather than the other way around. 'They were like women,
they never let on to the fact that they were taking over. I
mean, they are just like wives: they take command of you
[...]' He moves on to his next serious point, that dogs 'have

no big frontal lobes, just behind the forehead, such as we have.'

Extending his project of carrying through the task that the philosopher Immanuel Kant once set himself, to explain how the view that human beings have of the world is dictated by their biological makeup, Bronowski points out that:

> [The frontal lobes] make behaviour into patterns. They take the past and pattern it so that it is usable for the future. They organise behaviour [...] Man is able to make plans because the frontal lobes make it possible for him to take the past, rearrange it, hold it and use knowledge as potential power.

Science, he reminds us, is not merely a problem-solving activity or a matter of only making predictions, because the predictions have to fit into theories and laws that form long term strategies, and these can be formed because of the way our brains are made. Do scientific theories have a greater rigour than ethical judgements?

> The answer is that it takes you a lifetime to discover that neither of them has rigour. All that they have is a very great provisional strength: they have the power of knowledge you can act on.

'The twentieth century has something to be proud of, Western civilisation has something to be proud of,' declares Bronowski in the last of the broadcasts, going on:

> What? That it has taken the convictions of past centuries, that man is a profoundly imaginative and spiritual animal, and it has given them a foundation of scientific fact and theory which never existed before.

And if Western civilisation does not take the next steps in profound science, Bronowski recognises, those steps will be taken by people in Africa or China. 'If it happens, I won't drop a tear. I don't think it is anything very special that Euclid and Newton happen to have had white skins.' There were, indeed, no tears in the last broadcasts, but there was an autumnal feeling, and a sense of summing up, together with the boundless enthusiasm and optimism. Clearly, Bronowski as much as anyone knew that Western civilisation would only endure if it remained intellectually alive, and it saddened him to think that this might not turn out to be the case. Military power and economic might, whether in the 1970s or today, do not guarantee a place in the future.

Bronowski's optimism remains with us like a mountain-top visible through the shifting mists of fashionable pessimism because we have not really found anything with which to replace it. We can no more do without science than we can do without art, or indeed sex, which is, in human beings, as much fashioned by culture as by biology. In order to pass from our long childhood as a species to adulthood we need to have confidence in ourselves and the belief that we can change the world for the better. We need a sense of adventure and the faith that we *have* a future. We need to believe that we can ascend.

# List of Books and Articles

The dates and place names after the titles refer to the time and place of first publication.

## 1: Introduction: Bronowski's Footprints

Richard Leakey, Roger Lewin, *Origins Reconsidered* (London, 1992)
Germaine Greer, *The Female Eunuch* (London, 1970)

## 2: Full Heart and Full Mind: The Life

J. P. Stern, *Nietzsche* (London 1978 & 1985)
Martin Seymour-Smith, *Robert Graves: His Life and Work* (London, 1982, revised 1995)
Miranda Seymour, *Robert Graves: Life on the Edge* (London, 1995)
Richard Perceval Graves, *Robert Graves: The Years with Laura 1926-40* (London, 1990)
'Relative Interests' by Mathew Reisz, an interview with Lisa Jardine, *Times Higher Education,* January 17-23 2008
Letter to *The Times* by Eric and Freda Roll, August 1974
Michael Parkinson, *Parky: My Autobiography* (London, 2008)

## 3: Bronowski at Work: The Philosophy

Robert C. Tucker (editor), *The Marx-Engels Reader* (New York, 1978)
Mao Tsetung [sic], *Selected Readings from the Works of Mao Tsetung* (Foreign Languages Press, Peking [sic], 1971)
Friedrich Nietzsche, *Thus Spoke Zarathustra* (translated by R.J. Hollingdale, London, 1961, revised 1969)
Jean-Paul Sartre, *The Roads to Freedom* (translated by E. Sutton and G. Hopkins, London, 1947-50)
John Donne in *The Norton Anthology of English Literature* (New York and London, 1993)

Alexander Solzhenitsyn, *The First Circle* (translated by M. Hayward, M. Harari and M. Glenny, London, 1969)

Dylan Thomas, *Collected Poems 1934-1952* (London, 1952)

Eric Hobsbawm, *On History* (London, 1997)

'Failure is nothing to fear, says Rowling' article by Simon de Bruxelles, *The Times,* July 15 2000

A. & D. Lawson, *The Man Who Freed the Slaves* (London, 1962)

D. Z. Phillips, *Death and Immortality* (London, 1970)

Paul Addison, *Winston Churchill* (Oxford, 2007)

George Orwell, *The Collected Essays, Journalism and Letters* (edited by Sonia Orwell and Ian Angus, London, 1968, 1970)

George Orwell, *Nineteen Eighty-Four* (London, 1949)

F. R. Leavis, *The Great Tradition* (London, 1948)

## Works by Jacob Bronowski

*The Poet's Defence* (1939)

*William Blake: A Man Without a Mask* (1944)

*The Common Sense of Science* (1951)

*The Face of Violence* (1954)

*Science and Human Values* (1956)

*The Western Intellectual Tradition from Leonardo to Hegel* (with Bruce Mazlish, 1960)

*Biography of an Atom* (with Millicent Selsam, 1963)

*Insight* (1964)

*The Identity of Man* (1965)

*Nature and Knowledge: The Philosophy of Contemporary Science* (1969)

*William Blake and the Age of Revolution* (1972)

*The Ascent of Man* (1973)

*A Sense of the Future* (1977)

*Magic, Science and Civilisation* (1978)

*The Origins of Knowledge and Imagination* (1978)

*The Visionary Eye: Essays in the Arts, Literature and Science* (edited by Rita Bronowski and Piero E. Ariotti, 1978)

# Index